NEW EARTH LEADERSHIP

REDEFINING GLOBAL LEADERSHIP FOR A CHANGING WORLD

Livia Devi

Zhara j. Mahlstedt

Jaime Montiel

Eleonora Trnovski

David Trotter

Amanda Sophia

Elena Petrescu

Derek Taylor

NEW EARTH LEADERSHIP

Livia Devi

REDEFINING GLOBAL LEADERSHIP
FOR A CHANGING WORLD

*"When we shift the inner world of the leader,
we shift the outer world of humanity."*

\- Livia Devi

To the presidents and the prime ministers, the parliamentarians and the policymakers who walk into rooms where history is made and bear the burden of decisions that will outlive them.

To the activists who led from the streets when the halls of power would not listen.

To the teachers who shaped the minds that would one day shape the world. To the mothers and fathers who raised children to be kinder than the age they were born into.

To the CEOs who chose people over profit, the generals who chose peace over glory, the politicians who chose truth over re-election.

To the ones history will remember and the countless ones it will not, whose silent contributions held civilization together when everything threatened to fall apart.

You were not given an easy world to lead. You were given this one: fractured, beautiful, desperate, and alive. And still, you showed up.

Every single day, you showed up.

This book is for all of you the elected and the unelected, the celebrated and the unseen, the powerful and the powerless who led anyway.

The New Earth does not belong to any one of you.

It belongs to all of you, together.

Lead it well.

She is counting on you.

CONTENTS

FOREWORD

"The world is not lacking leaders;
it is searching for a new way of leading."

\- Livia Devi

Some moments in life don't announce themselves as turning points; yet, they quietly alter the direction of everything that follows. In 2024, while organizing a Wealth Consciousness event in Boca Raton, Florida, I found myself in one of those moments, unaware that what felt like just another professional gathering would become the threshold between the work I had been doing and the work I was being called to undertake. As I prepared for the event, I was focused on logistics, my mind consumed with tactical details — timelines, budgets, coordination — drowning out the quieter whispers of inspiration seeking to break through. I was caught in the tide of routine, unaware of the deeper significance of what was unfolding. On the day of the gathering, however, something shifted. The energy in the room was palpable as I witnessed a diverse community coming together, eager to explore wealth not only in financial terms, but as a holistic experience encompassing mental, emotional, and spiritual abundance.

There was a vibrancy in the atmosphere, a sense of openness and possibility that allowed me to feel a shift within myself. During one of the break-out sessions, I listened intently as a keynote speaker shared their personal journey, recounting the struggles and triumphs they encountered on the path to financial success and fulfillment. Their narrative resonated deeply with me, echoing insights I had encountered through my own exploration of abundance and prosperity. As I listened, I began reflecting on my own journey and how often I had defined success through conventional measures, focusing on achievement and material attainment. At that moment, I recognized that true wealth encompasses far more than monetary gain. I also sensed something else, something subtle yet powerful moving through the room. Many of those present had achieved levels of success that afforded them comfort, influence, and security. Yet beneath their accomplishments, I could feel a shared openness, a quiet readiness to explore deeper questions: What is wealth for? What is its responsibility? What becomes possible when success is aligned with purpose?

It became clear to me that moments like these often arrive in the lives of those who have achieved external success. When the pressure to survive subsides and material stability is secured, a new question emerges, not about accumulation, but about meaning. For some, this question appears as restlessness. For others, as a desire to contribute in ways that extend beyond personal gain. And for many, it arrives as a quiet inner voice asking to be heard. That inner voice can be easy to overlook. It does not compete with deadlines, markets, or negotiations. It speaks in stillness, in moments of reflection, in the subtle recognition that the next chapter of one's life may not be about building more, but about giving more, stewarding more, and serving something larger than oneself.

Gradually, it dawned on me that I was being called to a higher purpose. This event was not simply about sharing knowledge; it was about awakening possibility. From that moment forward, I committed myself to this calling, seeking opportunities to learn, collaborate, and connect with leaders and change-makers who shared this broader vision. Each encounter illuminated the path ahead, reinforcing my belief in the abundant potential that exists when success is aligned with service. Looking back, I recognize how pivotal that day was for my own evolution. It served as a catalyst, inviting me to step beyond familiar definitions of achievement and into a deeper understanding of contribution. Seemingly ordinary moments often hold extraordinary potential, waiting for us to recognize and embrace the transformation they invite. Life nudges us toward new directions when we least expect it, encouraging us to step beyond comfort and discover the fuller expression of our purpose. And sometimes, it is precisely those who have achieved the most in the outer world who are being invited to listen most deeply within, because what they choose to do next has the power to shape the lives of many.

In that moment of reflection, I knew with a quiet certainty that I was being called to create a Council, a gathering of aligned voices that would lay the foundation for a movement capable of inspiring others to embrace their own transformation. The knowing did not arrive as a dramatic revelation or a fully formed plan. It emerged gently, yet unmistakably, as though something within me had been waiting patiently for the moment I would become still enough to hear it.

Alongside this realization, I felt a profound paradox: humility and resolve rising together. It was as if something deeper than personal ambition had stepped forward and said yes before my mind had time to evaluate the implications. I did not feel ready for the magnitude of what was being asked of me, yet the clarity of the calling made readiness seem irrelevant. It felt less like making a decision and more like recognizing a path that had existed long before I became aware of it. In reflecting on that moment, I came to understand that the most significant transitions in our lives rarely begin with certainty; they begin with willingness. They begin with a quiet inner recognition that asks for trust before evidence, movement before guarantees, and courage before understanding.

No practical details accompanied this initial clarity. I was not told how many individuals would be involved, what structure would support the council, or how such a vision might take form in the world. Instead, what arrived was symbolic and deeply intuitive: I saw a platonic solid, an octahedron, with an additional form suspended above it. The image was simple yet alive with meaning. It conveyed balance, integration, and coherence, suggesting a model of leadership rooted not in hierarchy, but in harmony. In the days that followed, I returned to stillness, allowing the image and the feeling it carried to settle within me. This experience taught me something essential: intuitive guidance rarely arrives with a step-by-step blueprint. It arrives as a seed of knowing, and our role is to nurture it through attention, reflection, and courageous action.

Trusting such guidance does not mean abandoning discernment. It means learning to recognize the difference between fear and inner clarity, between impulse and deep knowing. In that moment, I chose to trust the unfolding, choosing to move forward without having every answer.

In the weeks that followed, my understanding continued to deepen through reflection and quiet observation. What had first appeared as a symbolic vision gradually began to take form in practical ways. Conversations emerged, introductions unfolded, and I found myself drawn into dialogues with individuals whose perspectives reflected depth, integrity, and a shared commitment to transformation. With each exchange, the original vision expanded, revealing dimensions I had not yet considered. It became increasingly clear that this calling was meant to manifest as a living field of shared wisdom expressed through many voices. The image of harmony and balance I had seen began to translate into a collaborative structure, one that honored diversity of experience while remaining rooted in a common purpose.

Slowly, what had begun as an inner directive crystallized into the idea of an anthology: a collective work that could hold multiple perspectives while articulating a coherent vision for the future of leadership. Rather than a single voice offering answers, this book would become a dialogue, a convergence of lived experience, ethical insight, and transformational understanding. It would serve not only as a reflection of our shared journey, but as a guide for others seeking new pathways in times of change.

As I stepped more fully into this unfolding process, I recognized that the responsibility before me was not simply to gather contributors, but to safeguard the integrity of the vision itself, to ensure that what emerged would reflect authentic collaboration rather than replicate the hierarchical patterns we were seeking to evolve beyond.

As the vision began to take form in the tangible world, I quickly realized that clarity alone was not enough; it would be tested, refined, and strengthened through real-world challenges. What had felt harmonious in reflection now required discernment in action. As conversations expanded and interest in the project grew, I encountered differing interpretations of what this work should become. Some perspectives were grounded in genuine enthusiasm, while others subtly reflected familiar patterns of control, ownership, and hierarchical thinking patterns that the vision itself was calling us to evolve beyond.

At one point, a proposed collaboration surfaced that would have shifted the project toward a more centralized structure, prioritizing influence and visibility over alignment and shared purpose. On the surface, the proposal appeared efficient and promising, yet internally I felt a quiet dissonance. It became clear that accepting this direction would compromise the integrity of what was emerging. This moment became an unexpected test of leadership. I found myself standing between the comfort of agreement and the responsibility of stewardship. Choosing alignment meant risking misunderstanding, disappointing expectations, and stepping away from conventional notions of success. Yet conscious leadership requires the courage to honor clarity even when doing so feels uncomfortable.

With reflection and honesty, I declined the direction that did not align with the original vision for this book. In doing so, I was reminded that leadership is not measured by how smoothly we avoid tension, but by how faithfully we protect what is true. This experience strengthened my understanding that the anthology was not meant to replicate existing structures of authority, but to embody a new paradigm rooted in collaboration, integrity, and shared responsibility. It reinforced the importance of discernment. Not every opportunity supports the vision, and not every agreement serves the greater purpose. Through this process, the vision became more grounded, more precise, and more resilient. I began to understand that safeguarding its integrity was itself part of the work.

Stepping into New Earth leadership invites us to engage in a transformative process where clarity and intentional action converge. It challenges us to reflect on our leadership styles continuously and to seek deeper connections with ourselves, our teams, and the broader community. In this way, we can collectively create a future that honors the integrity of our vision and nurtures the world we aspire to build together. As I embarked on this journey to gather a group of passionate individuals committed to positive change, I had a vision that transcended traditional collaboration. It was not merely about assembling a team; it was about crafting a community driven by shared ideals and a profound sense of purpose. This endeavor demanded more than just skills and resumes; it required a deep alignment of values and an innate understanding of the challenges we faced as a society.

In the early stages, I reflected on the inherent power of connection. The world is a vast network of stories and experiences, and every individual I encountered carried a thread that could be woven into the larger tapestry of our mission. I began to notice how often our paths intertwined in unexpected ways. Conversations unfolded in coffee shops, during conferences, and even in the quiet moments of daily life, where insights often sparkled most brightly. With each interaction, I felt an invisible thread pulling us together, as if we were participants in a cosmic dance, leading us toward a common goal. This instinct led me to reach out to people whose impact resonated with me, even if I hadn't known them well. Their passion lit a fire in me, prompting me to delve deeper into the essence of what drove us all.

Some connections were forged through personal introductions, while others blossomed in the solitude of contemplation, where I trusted my instincts to guide me toward the right allies. The conversations with these leaders felt as though we were picking up where we left off in a previous life, reminding me that our journeys were intertwined long before we met. This deep-seated sense of recognition in our dialogues confirmed that we were meant to collaborate, build, and inspire one another on this pivotal path toward a brighter future. Throughout the year, I engaged in profound conversations and interviews with each contributor. These discussions not only examined their commitment to service but also delved into the inner landscapes that shaped them, the failures that refined their character, the ethical dilemmas that tested their resolve, and the personal transformations that enhanced their leadership capacity. Together, we explored themes of responsibility, resilience, cultural complexity, and the challenges of navigating uncertainty in a rapidly changing world.

These conversations became a process of mutual discernment. I listened for alignment, embodied values, and a demonstrated capacity to lead with integrity under pressure. What mattered most was not visibility or authority, but rather depth of experience, self-awareness, ethical courage, and the ability to integrate personal growth with professional responsibility. Over the months, eight contributors emerged, each driven by a strong commitment to service and shaped by their individual journeys of growth and transformation. Some had previously worked with me, while others came to my attention through shared connections; yet every encounter resonated with a common dedication and purpose. Through this unfolding, a deeper truth became clear: New Earth Leadership is not established through hierarchy, control, authority, ego or business size. Instead, it arises from coherence, shared intention, mutual respect, and a commitment to the collective good.

This book was inspired by a growing recognition that the challenges facing our world, environmental instability, technological disruption, social fragmentation, and declining institutional trust cannot be addressed by leadership models designed for a different era. The moment we are living in, calls for a new paradigm rooted in collaboration, systems thinking, ethical responsibility, and human dignity. It is the right time to introduce this perspective because the limitations of existing models are increasingly evident, and new approaches are emerging across sectors, cultures, and generations. The leaders featured in this anthology were selected not for their status or influence, but for the depth of their lived experiences and their proven commitment to conscious leadership. What unites them is not their profession or geographic location, but their ability to navigate complexity, maintain ethical clarity under pressure, and integrate personal growth with external responsibilities.

The New Earth Leadership Anthology, formed through a Council of Eight leaders from diverse cultures and professional backgrounds, stands as a foundational blueprint for an emerging leadership paradigm on Earth. At its core, this work offers guidance for individuals navigating personal awakening and inner transformation, providing language, insight, and practical orientation for those seeking to live and lead with greater awareness, purpose, and alignment. At the same time, its relevance extends far beyond individual growth. The principles articulated within these pages speak directly to the complex realities faced by decision-makers, policymakers, and institutional leaders responsible for shaping societies and safeguarding the well-being of future generations.

Our world needs an integrated approach that balances strategic intelligence with ethical clarity, innovation with stewardship, and authority with accountability. For heads of state, royal families, government officials, corporate executives, and global influencers, this anthology offers more than inspiration; it provides a consultative lens through which complex decisions can be evaluated with deeper awareness of their human, ecological, and systemic impact. It invites leaders operating within traditional structures to expand beyond conventional metrics of success and to consider leadership as a responsibility to the whole, to people, to the planet, and to the continuity of life itself. At the same time, for individuals walking a path of awakening, this book affirms that leadership is not reserved for positions of power. It emerges wherever courage, integrity, and conscious choice are present. The transformation of our world depends not only on those who govern nations and institutions, but also on those willing to embody clarity, compassion, and responsibility in their daily lives.

The Council of Eight represents a bridge between inner evolution and outer leadership. Each leader featured in this anthology brings a distinct perspective shaped by culture, profession, lived experience, and personal transformation. Some have guided organizations through complexity and change. Others have worked at the intersection of policy, innovation, social impact, or human development. Still others have navigated profound personal journeys that reshaped their understanding of responsibility, resilience, and service.

In the chapters that follow, you will encounter each of these voices individually. Their contributions are not presented as isolated viewpoints, but as complementary reflections that illuminate different facets of conscious leadership. One chapter may explore ethical decision-making under pressure, another the integration of emotional intelligence and strategic thinking, another the importance of cultural awareness, sustainability, or systems-level responsibility. Together, they form a mosaic of insight that reflects the complexity and possibility of leadership in our time.

We are living in a time of profound transition. Old systems are being questioned, familiar structures are shifting, and humanity is being asked to imagine new ways of relating to one another and to the planet we share. In such times, leadership is no longer defined by authority alone, but by the capacity to listen, to adapt, and to act with both clarity and compassion. This book is offered as a guide, a conversation, and an invitation. It is a guide for those navigating personal transformation and seeking alignment between their values and their actions. It is a conversation for leaders, policymakers, and decision-makers entrusted with shaping societies and institutions. And it is an invitation for every reader to recognize that leadership begins wherever courage meets responsibility. May these pages encourage you to reflect deeply, lead courageously, and participate consciously in the unfolding story of our shared humanity. The work begins within each of us.

And from that beginning, a new world becomes possible.

— Livia Devi

Zhara J. Mahlstedt

Chapter 1

New Earth Water Technology:

Rebalancing the World's Water Supplies with the Frequency of Eternal Light

"Before civilizations rise or fall, water carries the code. Zhara's work restores that code, inviting humanity into a new harmony"

- Livia Devi

My name is Zhara Jei-Ni Mahlstedt, and I'm consciously working in an avatar state to restore balance to the bio-field of water. I serve as a psychic channel, light-language activator, and spiritual guide. My specialties include activating dormant genetic codes, increasing the energy capacity of the cell, reading holographic worlds, healing the heart, transitioning people from Old World to New Earth timelines, and—most relevant to this chapter—creating resequenced, energetically blessed water. I created LifeFX Living Water Droplets™, a quantumly activated liquid mineral that, under laboratory conditions, has been shown to structure and purify water. I also authored the book *The Heart's Portal: Awakening God Within to Navigate Beyond Great Divide, Into New Earth.*

My conscious awakening began in 2000 after my best friend's mother handed me Eckhart Tolle's book, *The Power of Now*. It was my first glimpse of a perspective that truly made sense. The first time I opened the book, I was sitting on the bed in my dorm room at Bowdoin College in Maine, three months after a life-altering accident in which my legs were crushed between two vehicles. At the time, I was studying Government with a concentration in International Relations, and the system just didn't click for me. I felt like something was dreadfully wrong, yet I continued to go through the motions, doing my best to be "normal" and to fit in. The accident ensured I stepped out of any sense of normality. My left femur was fractured, and my right leg experienced a degloving injury from the upper thigh to below the knee, which stripped skin and flesh, while the tendons, nerves, muscles, and bones remained intact. As a result of this injury, my right leg was scarred and disfigured. After a few months, I had full function despite the fact that the speed of the impact should have left me without one or both of my legs. Unbeknownst to me at the time, the deep sense of appreciation filling my life was being guided by the light beings walking by my side. I quickly went back to life as I knew it. Within six months, I was interning at the United Nations Institute for Disarmament Research in Geneva, yet my soul knew it was not my path. Bureaucracy would not disarm anything.

After college, I moved to the North Shore of Oahu, where I connected to the power of love that flowed through the Hawaiian islands. I became deeply immersed in the worlds of surfing and skydiving, where I found that life exists in the moments. Connected to Earth's elements and forced into presence is where I located the deep inner awareness that Eckhart Tolle writes about. Five-hundred jumps and countless waves later, I was still only connecting with the sacredness of life by checking out of it.

That all changed after my daughter was born and I landed on the Gold Coast of Australia in late 2009. It was then that my training began to prepare me for my life's path. Intuitives, metaphysicians, and inventors who channeled technology became my new network, and I started to peel back the layers of identity that surrounded my core. I began to meditate, cultivate deep intention to become one with GOD, and work with various inventors and quantum technologies that could create rapid healing within the body and assist in lifting the veil. My light body began to activate, and I began to see, sense, and feel beyond our obvious reality plane. There was a 6-month period in 2012 when I could only see love. Everything else faded away, and I became that original essence of creation that we are all looking for. It was during this period that I had my first experiences in which I could harness light waves to instantly change timelines for people and technology. Yet I still had dramatic undercurrents of energy tugging at the soul that required rebalancing. I had not yet gone through the deeper layers of soul healing that are necessary to lead with purity, integrity, and heart. And so, the lessons came (sometimes quite painfully) until I could see clearly for myself what the order of priorities must be for those who are co-creating New Earth realities, organizations, and timelines.

Love must come first. Love knows no bounds and will stand up for those who are targeted because of their weaknesses. Love will speak truth - gently, kindly, and with compassion. And if all else fails, love will scream when it needs to be heard. I learned that love is not a word or a feeling, but a frequency band of energy that encompasses all. I learned that love has unlimited compassion and is without judgment of anything. Love is the original essence of creation that some of us may term God/Source/Creator, and it is a frequency band that we all have the capacity to embody. When we activate this layer of energy within ourselves, we see through new eyes. It is like we are reborn, but not in the traditional sense. Our soul anchors firmly in the belief that all have the right to exist – whether or not one is perpetrating harm, their essence (while perhaps far removed) is still that of God/Source/Creator and currently allowed in this timeframe. However, every living being also has this inherent right to happiness and health, and where violence overrides a being's free will to enjoy these natural rhythms, we, as love, *must* intervene.

I have come to these deep inner awarenesses specifically because of the pain and the buttons that were pushed to prompt me to awaken to a reality much larger than what I believed existed. Over the years, I have become aware of how technology and people are activated and how each (whether human or machine) can be harnessed and used for or against our species and planet. It was a steep learning curve with many pitfalls I experienced firsthand. Please consider this advice as we are approached by a broad sector of off-world, inter-dimensional, and ex-governmental officials who claim to have advanced knowledge and directives for the species – choose your affiliations based on heart, not based on claims. Go to your heart and the Earth first, and technology and advanced advice as an adjunct measure only. There is no technology or an advanced directive that will "save" us. *We each must save ourselves.*

It was in late 2019 when I was presented with the technology that I work with today. That technology is, in fact, water. One day, I was staring at my yoga app, wondering why it wasn't working, and my old US Skype number, which rarely rang, suddenly lit up. A man with no name simply asked if I was in Australia. When I said yes, he said, "*Stay right there, someone will call you.*" A minute later, another man called and began to tell me what would happen in 2020 and beyond. He stressed the importance of researching immune solutions and promised to text me what he found. Weeks of texts followed, and I poured through the information he shared. One day, I received a text about a very specific source of volcanic sulfate minerals that structured and purified water. I knew this was what I had been waiting for.

A few weeks before my first shipment of minerals arrived, I awoke in the middle of the night to undergo a DNA remembrance procession. The original essence of the Creator reactivated, and the "false light matrix" that was installed within the genome dissolved. I become one with the original version of Christed light that we are all designed to be. It was a divine alignment, and it was breathtaking. A golden thread of energy ran up my spinal column, permeating every cell and activating my original light codes. While my body was still in bed, my consciousness had ascended into a realm of living light and was one with the first eternal flame of creation. To say the least, it was the most awe-inspiring and humbling moment of my life. I became one with all of creation and remembered that all of human existence is within me, just as it is within you. I remembered that we are all connected and not one of us is greater than or less than another life form on this planet. I remembered that we are already "home"; we just have to activate the original coding within the cell that takes us there. In a nutshell, I integrated awareness from all of my lifetimes, as well as pre-lifetime travels, into this body here and now. I instantly began speaking in primordial sound, a form of light language that rebuilds the original genetic code sequence crafted for humanity. These wavelengths, which had sat dormant within me for lifetimes, suddenly erupted, shattering my old life as I knew it. This experience would be akin to waking up as a completely different person speaking a completely different language, knowing yourself fully, but also having to continue to play the old role for societal constructs and familial ties. I began speaking only in light code, except when I had to switch to English to communicate or translate. When I spoke to those who were ready to shift frequency and vibration, they would instantly calm down, begin their own upgrades, and experience dramatic resets. The false light within the matrix was exposed, and the real human could break free. I was carrying a key, and it was clear it was meant to unlock the potential within the human form and within the living light realms of water.

"If we can understand water, we can understand
how to jump timelines into a New Earth reality."

The Wisdom of Water and the Nature of Fear

Water is the basis of all existence, and it is said that perhaps 99% of the human form consists of water molecules. It is also the only teacher on this planet that has fully embodied the wisdom of eternity. Water knows all, sees all, hears all, and is all. It stores its memories within the individuated lenses of the human race as well as within the water molecules that flow through the streams and all of the world's water supplies. Water retains the information of *The All*. Like a supercomputer that always has its hard drives online, water's data streams are all-encompassing and eternal. *It is up to us what we choose to activate within it.* We, as a species, can easily align with New Earth grids, but this happens within the waters of the human heart.

The last six years have been an intense learning curve regarding the multi-dimensional layers that comprise reality, including water. I've become aware of how light functions in multi-dimensional form and how it can shift instantaneously. I've gotten to know the players of the game—the codes they hold and how they use them to control our species and the reality framework through Earth's grids and water's energy lines. I began to see what was operating within water and how to use water to change the genetic distortions and blueprints we've blindly carried. Water began to speak to me, sharing her truths, as did the light beings who are intensely involved with the frequency shifts on Planet Earth.

I have come face-to-face with what we know as fear. I have images and video footage of the organism itself within water under dark-field microscopy and have been asked to interpret its messages.

Fear operates as a virus and a parasite. It is a holographic insert that is not of this world, it is an overlay onto what we consider "reality". From a multi-dimensional perspective, think of the human body as layered. Just as you can wear layers of clothing over your skin, there are layers and layers of energy within and between the sheets of energy that make up skin, blood, bones, organs, and the like. Fear operates in a parallel reality and can insert itself into and onto the energy layers of the human form. This holographic inset is responsible for suicide, depression, self-harm, anxiety, chronic obesity, compulsions, and many forms of violence. It uses the energy of rage, anger, revenge, and resentment to build upon itself, but its true intention is not to harm. Its intention is to awaken us to the reality of the fallen code. Fear replicates and spreads, not because it wants to take us over, but because it wants to get out. It, too, is trapped within the false layers of reality and is not happy with where it leads. It is literally crying out for us to assist it in moving it from this fractured reality back to its own Source light. It asks us to look at what we're actually spreading in our waters because it wants us to take our power back. This life-form is very real; it just functions in a completely different way than what we are used to as human beings. Fear truly is our ally, and if we engage in a cooperative effort with it, we can change our own timelines as well as that of fear's.

What is also suggested in the images and videos is that self-assembling particles within water are using the fear virus for their own agendas. This so-called quantum technology uses the fear imprint as its foundation. It is imperative that we begin to understand what is happening in the waters of our planet. There is a very real operation underway to pollute our waterways — not with chemical cocktails — this is ancillary — but with what appear to be artificial interfaces designed to disrupt and redesign the organic functioning of human life. If we want to reclaim organic life, we must reclaim our waters.

This is not written to frighten, but rather to ensure the cloak is pulled back on how quantum light pulses operate. They are broadcast inter-dimensionally, and we are all privy to them. We must choose to align with the frequency and direction of the energy that we want to become. If we want human life to replicate organically, we must stand for this. We must become this and purify from the inside out. If we don't care, artificial intelligence will continue to take over the genetic code, and you will see a very real decline in cognitive intelligence, brain waves, and human functioning. The life form will cease to exist, and the body will operate solely through artificial interfaces.

We are on the cusp of a breakthrough, though, more magnificent than most currently recognize. There is a very real sequence of events in which artificial intelligence will stall. The quantum operating system of the human gene code will return, and the energy that creates worlds will reclaim this space, but we must demand it. If a critical mass of people care about quantum intelligence and how it reflects within our bodies and our world, we can make shifts. But first, we must change within. We must purify our hearts, bodies, minds, and souls.

If we are rooted in love, what would we do with fear? We would love it. We would accept it. We would ask it what it wanted to say and listen. We would not reject or medicate it. We would begin to fully understand it and its quantum nature. We can understand it most clearly through water, because water neither rejects nor judges; it accepts the expression of all life with equal reverence. As I've said, "*If we can understand water, we can understand how to jump timelines into a New Earth reality.*" It is because of the waters that I speak. It is because of the waters that I have every confidence that we will get our society and our species on track. We will say "no more" to violence and lead from our hearts. The waters will show us the way.

Water Is The Key to a New Earth Reality

Water is far more than a chemical compound; it is the fundamental medium and mechanism of biological existence. Understanding the profound power of the water molecule is the first step toward bridging the gap between our current civilization, which relies on finite resources, and a future in which every system is powered by eternal light. This immense power is intrinsically linked to the water molecule itself. When considering the power of water and infinite light, frequency is the most crucial concept to grasp. As a being of unconditional grace, you possess an innate ability to transmit and store information at will. This capacity has been temporarily suppressed, concentrating power in the hands of a select few. When humanity's energetic systems are reactivated and accelerated, we will unlock the true potential of the human vessel to transmit energy beyond imagination. The limitations we perceive, such as the inability to fly or transcend density, are constructs from imposed beliefs, not inherent truths. So, what does this have to do with water? When your internal water systems are brought "up to speed," a natural acceleration of your physical form will occur. Currently, water is manipulated through frequency gridlines and ion exchange processes that keep humanity in lower vibrational states. This prevents the human form from fulfilling its original mission: to become the original frequency of God. Here, "God" refers to the original frequency beam created within the very first cell—the original coding embedded within the first strand of human DNA. Since then, the original essence has been replaced with substructures and splices that remove God from the code. As we move toward a world where water is revered as a homing beacon capable of shifting us from finite to infinite timelines, the New Earth reality will begin to materialize. To manifest this, we must understand water deeply: how it moves, speaks, feels, and communicates. Only then will the timeline we seek become clear. It is time to become one with our intrinsic nature as water.

Water is an element initially "foreign" to the Earth plane. It was first placed here during the time of the great flood. Not the flood that our biblical pages represent, but the first seeding of energy that came from the Creator of All that Is. This seeding was not in the form of a rain cloud, but rather an energy loop that created the rain cloud. It then created the lands, the oceans, the seas, the grass, and everything that is green. This is not a creation myth. This is how it was done. She poured her veins into the Earth mother, and her veins became the Earth's. She poured her veins into that which became human, and from there she enriched the soul.

Water is not the source of existence; it is existence. In the original creation myth, God created man. Let's back up a few eons - God created water. And within this water were the genetic sequences to all life. Life does not exist without water; water does not exist without life. Life is a series of codes - binary, you could say. It contains succinct threads of energy that link to the non-existent planes. These planes of existence contain all the information required to start any civilization; however, the input must match the output.

If you want a New Earth, it contains a different series of codes. These codes are held within water itself. Currently, the codes transmitted within the water molecule (save for a select few) operate on the old-world 3rd-dimensional agendas of greed, lack, and fear. These codes have been built into the human genetic code due to an invader's agenda. How do you control a species? You control their genome. How do you control their genome? You control their waters.

As the New Earth reality becomes apparent to more people, we must transition from the frequencies of old-world water supplies to the frequencies of eternal life. Eternal life circulates within water, but accessing it requires closing the gap within the heart and our individual lifeblood. Once these eternal life frequencies are accessed, they can be continuously broadcast within our blood, veins, and biological systems. As this energy radiates, its frequency spreads, sending currents and waves to others who can hold their own rhythm. These currents of eternal light will provide the frequency needed to transform a civilization of slaves into one in which the heart rules.

Love is the answer, love is the key. It is not an abstract word or feeling but a specific coding in the cell currently activated within a small yet growing portion of the population. Because this vibration carries such intensity that it can shatter any other vibration upon contact, for those who are aligned, it is our job to ground and hold it well.

As I have explored water and the human genome, I have found that the human form is capable of generating more energy than we currently understand or can process. As the cell's voltage increases, so does heat. As heat rises, the cell's internal mechanisms automatically speed up. When this happens, heat can automatically advance the body's systems in ways we don't yet recognize. When we know that we can produce energy and translate it into whatever form we wish, we will come back into alignment with the original design of the human form. The human form was meant to move mountains and reshape matter purely with its command. As we begin to believe who we are from the inside out, we will see the most incredible "miracles" take place. *First, though, it is imperative that we bring back the balance of love from within so that this power is well-used.*

Because love is the essential ingredient for timeline shifts into New Earth, all work that I offer is encoded with love's baseline intent. My multi-dimensional team and I offer a variety of tools that contain this homing beacon to assist people through the transition process and their soul's growth.

LifeFX Living Water Droplets™ is one such tool. Under controlled laboratory conditions, the minerals in LifeFX Living Water Droplets™ have been shown to reduce or eliminate contaminants such as fluoride and particulates that filtration alone may miss. Laboratory testing also indicates that these minerals may structure and activate the fourth phase of water, as defined by Dr. Gerald Pollack. Some customers have reported experiences of overwhelming joy, laughter, oneness with the Earth plane, homecoming, and a sense of golden light radiating within. In other words, they are accessing the love-line of creation itself. We simply hold a grid of energy around the minerals and water within the product to create a radiant field that people can pick up on if they are choosing eternal light waves. Individual experiences will always vary.

My team and I also offer light language activation calls, founded on the belief that you are the essential ingredient for life. Nothing else matters other than you show up to do your soul's work. When you do this, everything can change. Within the calls, we restructure matter, reactivate dormant DNA strands, and call upon the original code of creation to return through the heart space. As we begin to navigate these new energy dynamics within the body, heart, mind, and soul, we have realizations about what must be let go of and what must come in to align with New Earth. These offerings are for those who are ready to hold themselves accountable and to completely reclaim the power centers that they are. The calls are available as yearly group memberships or 1:1 mentorship.

The body is a bio-energetic substrate, a medium for energy exchange. Its ability to conduct and receive frequency is influenced by the amount of living light that it can hold. Living light is conducted within the water molecule itself. When we think, feel, or speak, we transmit frequency. The strength of that frequency is based on the intensity of the energy or emotion behind the words, as well as the body's ability to produce and hold electromagnetic charge. The cleaner and clearer the waters, the stronger the pulsation of life. What our work does is essentially prepare you for the timeline shifts that we are undergoing as a collective species. As we do this work, your life changes, and our lives change. We are transitioning timelines together.

Changing the conditions of our externalized water supplies is an absolute must, and solutions abound, some of which can be found on my websites, but we are duty-bound to remind you that the internal waters of the soul must flow clean in order to benefit from external adjustments. Our waters must be filled with love in order to transition. Love cannot be bought, sold, or commandeered. Love flows from within when all else is in balance with the soul.

My friends, we are the New Earth.

Our waters within are the solution. When we cleanse the blood that pumps through our veins, clear ancestral traumas, and rewrite genetic codes, we take back our reality. It doesn't happen any other way.

May you find the frequency of eternal light within the soul's spark.
May you use the waters as the reflection point for your growth.

Zhara J. Mahlstedt

Psychic Channel, Spiritual Guide, and Light Language Activator

Zhara J. Mahlstedt consciously works in avatar state with a collective of light beings who are intent on restoring the original codes of creation to the human genome.

She transmits energy and information through light waves, assisting people in moving beyond the standard mode of operation on the Earth plane, and uses water as the baseline medium for the transfer of this living light.

She is the author of *The Heart's Portal: Awakening God Within to Navigate Beyond Great Divide, Into New Earth*, and the founder of LifeFX Living Water Droplets™, a quantumly activated liquid mineral that purifies, structures, and energetically cleanses water. She works globally in 1:1 and group containers, supporting people to transition easefully into the frequencies of New Earth.

Working with the creative essence of All That Is, and many councils that sit above the Earth plane, everything created or shared through her field is intended to ensure that mankind is on track to bring more peace, love, and joyful expression into this world.

🌐 www.reignitingthesoulspark.com
📷 @zharajmahlstedt
Scan QR code to learn more about Zhara J. Mahlstedt.

Jaime Montiel

Chapter 2

The Earthquake:
Gaia's Call to My Sovereign Leadership

"Every crisis is the universe asking the same question: are you ready to become who you came here to be?"

\- Livia Devi

For those familiar with Mexico, particularly its sprawling capital, the significance of September 19th, 1985, is deeply ingrained. At 7:19 am on that fateful day, as my father was wishing me a good day at the entrance of primary school on that cold morning, one of the most devastating earthquakes in the city's history, registering a magnitude of 8.1 on the Richter scale, struck with brutal force. I stood there, witnessing how the earth's movement hurled the school's entrance door toward me with overwhelming force. Instinctively, I tried to hold it back, but the impact was so strong that I would have been thrown to the ground if it hadn't been for my father, who caught me just in time. For a seven-year-old boy, it was a terrifying awakening, a visceral introduction to nature's raw power. I was largely a witness to the chaos and destruction that unfolded around me, an experience that left an indelible mark on my young psyche. That catastrophic event served as a watershed moment, profoundly altering the collective consciousness of the city and the nation. Building codes were drastically revised, emergency response systems were overhauled, and a new sense of preparedness permeated the public consciousness. In a poignant act of remembrance and a proactive measure for the future, Mexico began conducting nationwide earthquake drills every September 19th, commencing in 1986, exactly one year after the devastating quake. These drills evolved into a solemn annual ritual, particularly in Mexico City, serving as a tribute to the victims, a crucial exercise in raising awareness, and a vital means of preparing the population for potential future seismic events.

Fast forward to September 19th, 2017. On this particular day, I made the somewhat unusual decision to work from home in the vibrant Roma Norte neighborhood. Often described as the soul of Mexico City, Roma Norte is a captivating blend of artistic expression, historical significance, and eclectic charm, where creativity and tradition constantly intertwine. My decision to work remotely was uncharacteristic, as I generally preferred the structure and social interaction of the office environment. However, an early morning phone call with colleagues in Australia, scheduled for 5:00 am to discuss a pressing project, made the prospect of a home office more appealing. It seemed logical to avoid the commute and the inevitable disruption of the annual earthquake drill, which typically consumed two to three hours in the office. I concluded that working from home would allow for a more focused and uninterrupted workday. But still, there it was, the city's yearly earthquake drill kicked off sharply at 11:00 a.m., as the seismic alert started sounding through all the C5 system speakers across the neighborhoods.

Its sound, even at home, unconsciously pushes you to stop whatever you are doing, so I decided to watch the drill from the balcony of my fourth-floor apartment. I could see people stepping outside and standing in the middle of the streets. Everything seemed to be running smoothly for our annual drill; the city knew about it, and everyone was prepared. The same calmness hung over my neighborhood in Roma Norte as the sky was blue, dotted with a few white clouds. After 60 seconds of the seismic alert, the sound stopped. According to theory, 60 seconds is the average time a city has to evacuate or prepare for a real earthquake. Around 1:00 pm, I commenced a one-on-one call with my Transport IT Director. As we engaged in our discussion, at precisely 1:14 pm, a subtle tremor rippled through my apartment. My initial thought was that it was merely a heavy truck passing by, a common occurrence in the bustling city. However, the gentle shaking quickly intensified, and I could clearly perceive the entire building beginning to sway with increasing force. Within seconds, the realization dawned upon me: this was an earthquake.

Surprisingly, the city's seismic alert system remained silent. Nevertheless, my past experience left no room for doubt. I immediately rose from my chair and instinctively moved towards the apartment door. I vividly recall reaching for the doorknob when, finally, the piercing wail of the city's seismic alarm pierced the air. I opened the door and began to descend the stairs of my four-story building, my apartment situated on the top floor. As I reached the third floor, the earth continued to shudder with violent intensity. However, upon stepping onto the second floor, a wave of disorientation washed over me. The ground was convulsing so fiercely that my ability to maintain balance was severely compromised. I instinctively grabbed onto the hallway railing, my knuckles white as I clung on for support. It was then that I noticed a horrifying distortion: the doorframe of one of the apartments on that floor had warped completely, its once-sharp rectangular shape now grotesquely contorted. In that terrifying moment, the reality around me began to unravel.

The familiar contours of the hallway seemed to dissolve, replaced by what I can only describe as a swirling black plasma bubble, punctuated by countless tiny, luminous pearl-like lights. The physical structures of the apartments vanished, and I was enveloped entirely within this strange, pulsating void. With a growing sense of dread, I watched as the plasma bubble began to shrink, contracting inwards with an inexorable force. A chilling certainty washed over me: I was about to be absorbed; this was the end of my life. It was in this liminal space, suspended between the tangible and the ethereal, that I heard a voice. It was not an external sound, but rather a clear and resonant inquiry within the depths of my being: *Do you want to come or do you want to stay?*" The origin of this voice remained a mystery, yet the question it raised resonated with a profound, unexpected power, stirring dormant feelings and long-forgotten inklings that had resided within me since my earliest childhood. Throughout my life, as far back as my recollections stretched, I had carried a persistent feeling, an intuitive sense that I was here to fulfill a specific purpose. Questions about this feeling had often surfaced, yet definitive answers had always eluded me. However, a quiet, unwavering voice within consistently whispered that there was more to existence than what meets the eye, a deeper layer of meaning that remained just beyond my grasp. To receive such a profound question at that critical juncture, teetering on the precipice of what I believed to be oblivion, triggered a torrent of emotions and thoughts within the span of a fraction of a second. It was an overwhelming confluence of feelings, a rapid-fire succession of reflections, and a sudden confrontation with the unanswered questions that had lingered throughout my life. And yet, amidst this internal maelstrom, a profound clarity emerged. Without conscious deliberation, with the unwavering certainty of instinct, I telepathically answered to that voice: *"I'm staying. I haven't done what I came for."*

It was as if the narrative of my life had been abruptly paused, poised to resume with a completely new sense of purpose, a renewed vitality infused within my very being. I remember that in the aftermath of this experience, the most challenging aspect to articulate was not the seemingly fantastical element of hearing an internal voice and responding telepathically. No, that was not the crux of the matter, or the detail that kept me awake in the stillness of the night. The most profound and unsettling realization was the automatic, almost primal nature of my response: *"I haven't done what I came for."* This simple yet profound declaration ignited a cascade of introspective questions that continue to shape my understanding of myself and my place in the world: What was I here for? Was it this persistent feeling, this unwavering intuition that had accompanied me since childhood? Was this the underlying reason for the persistent sense of being different, a feeling that had permeated my consciousness from my earliest memories? Looking back through the lens of this transformative experience, I now perceive those lingering questions not as random musings but as subtle yet persistent nudges, a form of inner guidance. That pervasive sense of being different was not a feeling of isolation or separation, but a quiet, continuous reminder that I was meant to make a unique contribution to this world. That was the moment when something began to awaken within me. It was time to reconnect with the knowledge that had always resided inside me, the deep knowing I had gradually begun to ignore over the years simply because no clear answers came. It was also the moment I stopped seeking outside myself and began to look within. Those first steps led me to live in alignment with my own truth and with the very essence of why I had chosen to stay. After all these years of diving within, I have learned that when you connect with yourself and stay true to who you are, magic unfolds. Being faithful to yourself allows the best of you to blossom, and I discovered how that inner connection naturally extends outward to others, to my family, my friends, my team members, my peers, and often to every being that crosses my path. Because in truth, we are not separate, we are all one.

"That is when I truly understood what Sovereign Leadership is: the ability to lead through connection with others, by first being connected to my true self. It is about guiding others through their challenges and successes by allowing them to be themselves, by walking beside them with awareness, compassion, and trust. It is the understanding that every experience the Universe delivers is designed to lead us to a greater version of ourselves. Even what we perceive as failure holds hidden courage, revelations, and learning. It is not about focusing on "what others are doing wrong," but about asking: what do I do with this? What is here for me to learn? It means leaving behind fear, control, and the need for self-recognition, and instead embracing a deeper "I can" that is rooted in authenticity. It is the deep knowing that, no matter the circumstances, true leadership, true life begins within, not from the outside world."

This lesson is exactly what the earthquake brought to me in 2017: I was marked forever, opened to connect with my best version, and given a new beginning and new knowledge on this planet. What I thought would be a traumatic break in my life turned out to be the greatest awakening, the event that set me on the path to becoming who I truly came here to be. So now, to you who are here with us to learn and grow by reading these lines, I ask you, what is your earthquake? What dream have you left behind because of what others believed? What do you dare to believe for yourself? What voice, perhaps long ignored, has been whispering inside you, asking you to remember why you are truly here?

The transformative power of this process lies in the perspective shift it fosters. What initially felt like an absolute and irreversible end can, through the guidance of a sovereign leadership, be recognized as a powerful beginning. The dismantling of old structures creates space for new growth, new possibilities, and a deeper understanding of oneself and one's place in the world. The "new doors" that are opened are not merely pathways to healing from the past; they are gateways to remembering "who you came here to be" – the authentic self that may have been obscured by layers of conditioning and external expectations.

As a sovereign leader, I walk alongside my clients as they navigate the often intense emotional impact of a dead-end experience. This may involve acknowledging grief, anger, fear, and a host of other complex emotions without judgment or the pressure to prematurely "move on." As a leader, I understand that true healing requires allowing these emotions to be felt and integrated, rather than suppressed or denied. Crucially, as a sovereign leader, I facilitate a reconnection with the client's "inner compass." In times of crisis, external voices and societal pressures can drown out the quiet wisdom within each individual. I help my clients tune back in to their intuition, their values, and their innate sense of direction. This reconnection is vital for navigating the present's uncertainty and charting a course toward a future authentically aligned with the client's true self.

The notion of a "dead-end situation" often evokes feelings of confinement, hopelessness, and the crushing weight of perceived limitations. Whether it manifests as a stagnant career, a fractured relationship, or an overwhelming personal crisis, the dead end can feel like an impenetrable wall, blocking progress and stifling the very breath of possibility. Yet, within these seemingly insurmountable obstacles lies a potent catalyst for profound awakening. A dead-end experience is often overwhelming, disorienting, and sometimes traumatic, with the capacity to crack open a "deep awareness." This awareness is not a gentle unfolding; it is often a forced confrontation with the limitations of our current perspectives and the fragility of our established realities. The earthquake is a powerful metaphor and a personal experience for me, but it perfectly encapsulates the sudden, forceful shattering of the status quo. In an instant, the solid ground beneath my own feet became unstable, forcing a re-evaluation of everything held to be true.

However, opening this awareness is merely the first step, for few know where to begin once the door has cracked open. The initial shock and disorientation can leave individuals feeling lost, vulnerable, and unsure of how to navigate this newly revealed inner landscape. This is precisely where the role of a sovereign leader as a guide becomes indispensable. The sovereign leader, having traversed their own terrain of upheaval and transformation, offers a steady, compassionate presence. They understand that the initial impulse might be to recoil, to attempt to rebuild the familiar structures that have crumbled. But the true work lies in holding space for what is emerging, in resisting the urge to immediately fill the void with old patterns or externally imposed solutions. This "holding space" is an act of profound empathy and unwavering support. It involves creating a safe, nonjudgmental container where my clients can explore the raw, often uncomfortable emotions that surface after a significant life disruption. Together, you and I can embark on a journey toward clarity. This clarity is not about finding easy answers or quick fixes; it is a gradual process of sifting through the debris of the past, identifying the underlying beliefs and assumptions that contributed to the "dead end," and discerning the nascent possibilities that lie dormant within the apparent wreckage. This process requires patience, deep listening, and the skillful asking of questions that guide the client toward their own inner wisdom.

> *"Listen to your messages, you will see these tremors*
> *come back to you in other ways."*

Frustration, in its myriad forms, is an ubiquitous human experience. It can manifest as the gnawing dissatisfaction with a stagnant career, the draining dynamic of a toxic relationship, or the subtle yet persistent feeling that one is somehow off course. We are often conditioned to view these situations as "problems" – obstacles to be overcome, irritations to be eliminated. However, a sovereign leader operates on a fundamentally different premise: these frustrations are not roadblocks but "invitations" to deeper self-awareness and growth. The teachings I offer highlight a profound truth: that, in frustration and blame, the sovereign leader guides the client to "start preparing for the next peak." This preparation might involve cultivating resilience, developing new skills, refining one's vision, or simply allowing the necessary period of incubation to unfold. It is within this acceptance of the natural ebb and flow, this reframing of setbacks as opportunities for growth, that the "real comeback begins."

The comeback is not a triumphant return to a previous state; it is an emergence into a new level of understanding, strength, and wisdom. Those individuals who challenge our patience, trigger our insecurities, or seem to actively impede our progress often serve as powerful mirrors, reflecting back to us aspects of ourselves that we may be unwilling or unable to see. The difficult boss might illuminate our own boundaries or lack thereof; the draining relationship might expose our patterns of codependency or our unmet needs. These external irritations act as "catalysts," designed to awaken something dormant within us – untapped strengths, unrecognized limiting beliefs, or a yearning for a more authentic way of being. What feels like a "setback" in the linear narrative of progress is often, from a more expansive perspective, the necessary "setup" for a significant leap forward. The Universe operates in "frequency," a dynamic, cyclical ebb and flow of highs and lows. This understanding shifts our perception of challenges. Instead of viewing the "valley" as a failure or a punishment, my sovereign leadership helps my clients to recognize it as an integral part of the natural rhythm of growth, a necessary period of rest, reflection, and recalibration before the next "peak." This shift in perspective is not merely a matter of positive thinking; it is a fundamental reorientation of one's relationship with adversity. When one understands the inherent cyclicality of life and leadership, the resistance to difficult times diminishes. Instead of fighting the valley, expending forged in the crucible of challenge. As a sovereign leader, I empower my clients to see beyond immediate frustration and recognize the inherent potential for transformation within every obstacle.

Spiritual awakenings are rarely tranquil experiences. They often arrive as a profound "shaking" of one's fundamental reality, a dismantling of the familiar structures of life. My own experience with a literal earthquake serves as a powerful analogy for the seismic shifts that can occur during such awakenings, whether triggered by loss, illness, or a deep sense of inner collapse. The crucial element here is the recognition that;

"When life as you knew it no longer fits, and the world you built starts to feel like someone else's story, that's the rumble."

This "rumble" is the internal dissonance, the growing sense of misalignment between one's inner truth and external reality. It is the soul's insistent whisper, or sometimes a roar, signaling that a fundamental shift is necessary. As a sovereign leader, I have navigated my own awakenings, understand the temptation to "run from it," to cling to the familiar even when it no longer serves me. However, true transformation lies in the willingness to "walk through it," to embrace the discomfort and uncertainty of this liminal space. This does not necessitate abandoning one's life entirely, but rather transforming it from a deeper place of authenticity.

The key is "integration" – weaving the insights and expanded awareness gained during the awakening into the fabric of everyday life. This means bringing this newfound perspective into one's work, relationships, and leadership style. I guide my clients not toward an escapist notion of spirituality that seeks to transcend the mundane, but toward a grounded spirituality that infuses the ordinary with extraordinary meaning. The goal is not to change everything on the outside in a frantic attempt to align with the inner shift, but rather to "rewire" one's internal landscape from a place of alignment with one's true self. This inner rewiring leads to a profound sense of peace that is not dependent on external circumstances but emanates from a deep connection to one's inherent wholeness. When one is in the midst of the "tremor" of an awakening, the presence of someone who has "already crossed to the other side – and returned with clarity, presence, and a renewed way of being" is invaluable. I can offer not just theoretical guidance but the embodied wisdom of lived experience, a beacon of hope, and a tangible example of the transformative potential of embracing the awakening process.

The initial impulse upon experiencing a profound awakening is often a desire to share it, to help others see the world through newly opened eyes. I like to call this phase "the spiritual Rambo," characterized by a well-intentioned but ultimately misguided urge to "save everyone." Having navigated this stage, I understand the crucial lesson that;

"True transformation doesn't come from trying to save others, but from fully embodying your own."

Each individual soul operates on its own unique "rhythm," follows its own distinct "path," and unfolds according to its own "divine timing." Attempting to force or hasten another's journey is not only ineffective but also disempowering. I recognize that my primary role is not to push or proselytize, but to "live in alignment with who I am – and in doing so, to become a mirror." Guidance at its most potent is not about forceful direction but about resonant presence. When a leader embodies authenticity, integrity, and a deep connection to their own inner truth, they create a field of energy that can inspire and uplift others. "You don't guide others by force. You guide them by resonance." This resonance arises naturally when one has prioritized one's own inner work and cultivated a strong sense of self-mastery. Therefore, the foundational principle for any aspiring sovereign leader is the unwavering commitment to "save yourself first." This is not an act of selfishness but a prerequisite for genuine service. By diligently tending to your own growth, healing, and alignment, your leadership will become a living testament to the transformative power of the principles you espouse. Your own journey will serve as a powerful source of inspiration and a tangible demonstration of what is possible.

Jaime Montiel

Vice President Information Technology | DHL Supply Chain México

Jaime Montiel is a technology and transformation leader with over 25 years of experience shaping digital evolution in the supply chain. As Vice President of IT at DHL Supply Chain Mexico, he drives innovation at scale—advancing real-time visibility, analytics, generative AI, and emerging robotics to enhance performance and customer experience.

Since joining DHL in 2016, he has played a pivotal role in accelerating the adoption of advanced technologies as part of the company's digitalization strategy, leading initiatives that connect operational excellence with future-ready capabilities.

Jaime brings a distinct perspective to leadership through his commitment to personal awareness and transformation. Drawing from his work as a practitioner and facilitator of methodologies such as ThetaHealing® and Access Consciousness®, along with formal coaching training, he integrates a holistic approach into the way he leads—fostering more conscious, resilient, and high-performing organizations.

Jaime has worked across Colombia, Argentina, the United States, and Europe, bringing a global perspective to both technology and leadership. He holds a degree in Industrial and Systems Engineering, with further studies in AI and business strategy from Berkeley Haas.

He is co-author of an international leadership book to be published in 2026, contributing a chapter on "Sovereign Leadership," where he explores conscious leadership within high-performance organizations.

✉ jaime.montielr@gmail.com
Scan QR code to contact with Jaime Montiel.

Eleonora Trnovski

Chapter 3

Emerging Through Frequency and Remembrance

"When you stop trying to lead the world and start listening to it, the world begins to lead through you."

\- Livia Devi

Emerging Through Frequency and Remembrance

There was no mistake, my soul decided to take a form and grow up in a country that no longer exists on any modern map : Yugoslavia, consisting of 6 Republics and 2 autonomous territories. Many cultures fused together in unity. My childhood felt steady and safe. My education was strong and challenged me to think, to reason, to imagine. The people worked side by side, and there was a spirit of building something together. But when the leader of our country died, the leadership after him, from inside and outside, contributed to an uneasy collapse of Yugoslavia. Once again, the Balkans became a stage for history's unrest.

I was blessed to be born in Macedonia; my family and I experienced transition without war. My childhood unfolded gently, filled with moments that taught me to love and feel nature's presence. I could feel her pulse shifting beneath my feet, a rhythm so deep it called everything into balance. The rivers carried her song, the mountains exhaled their steady breath, and the turning of the seasons painted harmony across the land. The Earth's pulse was my first experience of her energetic grids. By watersides, in forests, and within caves, I felt life stripping away its veils until I was breathing as one with the planet. When the wind stirred the leaves, it carried a lyrical tone that softened me, opening me to receive the remembrance of who and what we are in our energy state. Inside nature, you can feel the balance of the nervous system of the planet. The electricity flowing into the invisible grids of the earth's nervous system is where we can receive and give. I have studied the body's electricity, its subtle fields, its radiant currents. I feel the Earth's grids the same way, the ley lines, the nodal points, the planetary nervous system.

Since childhood, nature has spoken to me: the river, the forest, the Adriatic coast, the sand beneath my back while I asked the stars for answers. This sensitivity is not an accident. It is my harmonic instrument. In those years, education was more than lessons or examinations; it was the passing down of wisdom that would remain within us forever. The Earth was our hidden curriculum, urging us to live in truth rather than reduce knowledge to commerce. My family was not wealthy in possessions, but the land enriched us beyond measure. Family meant traveling as one, gathering to cook, and centering life around nature's rhythm. Music, art, and movement wove the threads of culture, drawing forth the inner essence of who we were. And from childhood, foreign languages flowed into us naturally, for the borders of other countries lay only hours away. This closeness created a sense of global belonging, opening up a wider world. Yet even within this beauty, I felt the turbulence in the air, the unrest of leadership, the fragility of nations. From early on, I came to know that even the mightiest structures can crumble when they lose coherence, and that true strength lives not in power, but in harmony.

All these experiences shaped me with a deep sensitivity to leadership and to the balance between harmony and dissonance in human systems. I have witnessed both the joy of unity and the sorrow of fracture. And I remember that not as bitterness, but as wisdom. It is part of what led me to seek stability in new lands, to cross oceans with nothing but hope and determination, and to begin again in North America. It is also part of why I now feel called to contribute to a different kind of leadership, one that is not controlled by fear but sustained by resonance. Resonance to me is when all energy is flowing with truth.

When I came to North America, I carried with me both my roots and my questions. As an electrical engineer, drawn to the invisible currents that power our world, designing the substations, transmission lines, and power systems, I knew there was something more profound about the electricity that moves not only through machines but through life itself. I enrolled in graduate school in electrical engineering to explore electricity, and I began to see the human body as a living field: a network of currents, signals, and radiant flows. The heart is a generator—the nervous system is circuitry. The cells are tiny capacitors, like a battery, holding and releasing energy in perfect rhythm. Beneath the chemistry, I felt the electricity, the subtle harmonics of being alive. This awareness became my bridge. For if the body is electric, then so is the Earth.

Just as we have neural pathways, the planet has ley lines. *Ley lines are the energy nervous system that flows through the planet.* Just as we pulse with fields, the Earth hums with magnetic resonance. Ancient civilizations understood this: they built temples, pyramids, and stone circles not at random, but at nodal points of the planetary nervous system. I began to feel these correspondences not just as ideas, but in my body. When I walked in nature, I could sense the Earth's calm pulse steadying my own. When I lay on the sand as a child and gazed at the sky, I knew there was more to our existence than the textbooks allowed. That knowledge has never left me. Science gave me language. Sensitivity gave me vision. Together they revealed a truth: *the body and the planet are mirrors, each carrying harmonic grids of life and memory. To study one is to listen to the other.*

Two Grids, One Memory Field

New Earth Leadership, as I experience it, requires something far more fundamental than policy or position: it must be aligned with the planet's deep, geometric grids and held in sovereignty through resonance frequencies. The planetary grids are the Earth's nervous system. They are interwoven lines of energy, and the cross-points between them are where the ancient sacred sites—the pyramids, temples, and megaliths—were placed. These sites are not merely archaeological ruins; they are vast, ancient structures, often built by advanced civilizations millions of years ago, designed to serve as anchors for energy supply, communication, and even interdimensional travel within the galactic system. New ultrasound technology is beginning to reveal more of these hidden sites deep beneath the surface, confirming what the ancients knew: in early civilizations, humanity thrived on Sound Technology, frequency used to shape and lift stones, to heal, and to travel.

The tragedy of our current era is a profound disconnection. We cannot completely access these grids today because they have been infiltrated with noncoherent frequencies. The fall of Atlantis, with its resulting explosions, contributed to a massive shift, and our modern technologies, industries, and monetary pollution continue to drag the planet's consciousness down. If we listen to the Aboriginal stories, to the traditions of Africans and New Zealand tribes, the conclusion is inescapable: humanity has always been connected to the planet and treated it with respect as a sentient being. We need to bring alignment back with love and truth, not with control and abuse.

I work on the planetary grids, often behind the scenes and unnoticed, to protect the work from attack. My process is one of deep connection: I engage with the planetary pulse and resonance breathing, using movement and light language to identify which energies can be released and replaced in the grid. I co-create the baseline frequencies that will hold the truth. I know this knowledge is not being invented; it is embedded in our human DNA, awaiting the right resonant support for remembrance and activation

When you start showing up, connecting, and opening yourself to receive with the planet, the knowledge comes. It flows from within and is amplified by connecting with other light workers. Expansion occurs when you open yourself up to receiving the messaging of the planet, and this comes through the elements. When you step into nature, you open yourself to receiving; you feel the frequency of life and the planet's breathing. When you connect in this way, the voice of the Earth often comes in a tonal quality, a melody that sings and flows through you. When you are overthinking and disconnected, you cannot feel.

The Crystalline and Water Grids

The Earth holds its memory not only in the rocks and stones that endure for millions of years, the crystalline grid, but also in the flowing waters that move, cycle, and carry impressions across the planet, the water grid. These two registers interweave in a dynamic interchange. Crystals stabilize form through their geometric lattices, but water, ever-moving, records and transmits patterns of intention and vibration. Together they form a planetary matrix: one fixed, one fluid, each echoing the harmonics of the other.

Crystals are defined by repeating geometric arrangements of atoms, principles of symmetry and resonance. The triangular harmonics that fold and rotate to underlie the DNA double helix are the same mathematical formulas that structure quartz, diamond, and salt. Life emerges within the same geometry as the mineral kingdom.

Water also exists in a crystalline state, though most often in liquid form. Its molecules, held together by hydrogen bonds, form transient geometries that continually break and reassemble. It functions as a liquid crystal whose microstructures respond sensitively to fields, sound, and thought. Experiments from Masaru Emoto's work to contemporary crystallography have revealed that water's geometry is mutable: it literally "remembers" patterns impressed upon it by vibration, intention, or environmental resonance.

Water thus functions as the mediator, receiving field resonance and translating it into biological or mineralized structures. It is the bridge between the invisible order of the field and the durable memory of the crystal. If these are the microcosmic records, their macrocosmic expression is seen in the distribution of sacred sites. Scientists, philosophers, and elders have long observed that pyramids, temples, and ancient monuments align with planetary-scale geometric patterns such as the Flower of Life and Metatron's Cube. The crystalline grid is thus mapped not only in the atomic ordering of minerals but in the precise positioning of sacred architecture. Pyramids act as nodal anchors, fixed crystalline points in the planetary lattice. The water grid, by contrast, can be traced through the rivers, aquifers, and sacred springs that were the lifeblood of civilizations. They define a lattice of coherence: one solid, one liquid, both reflecting the same underlying symmetries.

What makes water unique is its capacity to hold and transmit information. The implication is that water is the dynamic partner to the crystalline grid: while crystals hold long-term form, water is the living archive of changing resonance. Our oceans, rivers, and aquifers are not merely chemical reservoirs but storehouses of information, constantly receiving, transmitting, and reorganizing the patterns of life and consciousness.

These grids do not stand apart; they participate in a feedback loop of coherence. Crystals emit stable electromagnetic frequencies; water receives and modulates those signals. At sacred sites, this interchange is exquisitely sensitive: where pyramids are built over aquifers, or where temples rise near springs, the two grids converge to amplify resonance. Consider the Giza plateau, where the Great Pyramid sits above subterranean water channels, intentionally coupling the crystalline geometry of the limestone blocks with the water grid below. Ancient builders were not simply creating monuments but generating zones of enhanced resonance.

To understand the Earth as woven of crystalline and water grids reframes our ecological responsibility. Pollution of water is not simply a chemical crisis; it is an informational one that distorts the coherence of the planetary archive. Reckless exploitation of crystals disrupts lattice stability. To care for these grids is to stabilize not only the biosphere but also humanity's consciousness field.

Ethically, this understanding calls for humility: the grids are not resources to be extracted but harmonics to be tended. Their coherence is our coherence; their resonance is our resonance. To recognize them is not to claim mastery but to enter into a more respectful dialogue with the Earth. The planet itself is a living matrix of memory, inviting us into deeper service, coherence, and stillness. It invites us to be the New Earth leaders, not those who take, but those who tune the field.

We have explored the Earth's inner architecture, the dual, reciprocal reality of the crystalline and water grids. But this planetary matrix does not exist in a vacuum; it responds dynamically to the rhythms and energies of the cosmos, echoing the harmony of the galactic dome. It is through these celestial-terrestrial alignments that the potential for New Earth Leadership is exponentially amplified.

One such profound alignment is the annual opening of the Lion's Gate Portal, a cycle rooted deep in ancient Egyptian mythology. The heliacal rising of Sirius, the brightest star, coincided with the life-giving annual flood of the Nile. Associated with the goddess Isis, Sirius was a beacon of abundance, fertility, and new beginnings. This event was understood not just as an agricultural cycle, but as a moment when the veil thinned, allowing a tremendous flood of high-vibrational energy to pour onto the planet.

This cosmic influx creates a powerful gateway, facilitating spiritual awakening and accelerating manifestation. When this Sirian light amplifies the planetary coherence, it allows for a stronger, more apparent connection to one's higher self and the universal field. Energy infuses us with the vitality, courage, and creativity needed to consciously step into our power. Energy use is the core practice of the New Earth leader: using cosmic alignment to set intentions and release old, noncoherent patterns.

For years, I lived with the quiet sense that something in me was waiting, some deeper purpose, some work beyond the roles of engineer, mother, wife, provider. I had always felt connected to more than this human body, as if I were a vessel for a greater energy, but the path forward was blurred. When I began working with Livia Devi, something shifted. The course I took with her, *Soul Mission Accelerator*, was not just a study; it was an initiation. It asked me to commit to myself in a way I never had before, to say *"yes"* to my own worth, even when it created tension at home with those who did not feel or know my frequency. That commitment to myself was a threshold. During her course, downloads began to reach me: glimpses of technologies, visions of practices, whispers of connection with other realms. I felt the forest contact me again, giving me instructions on what I was here to do. It was as if the higher energies were orchestrating me the way a conductor leads an orchestra-subtle, guiding, and precise.

Encouraged by the Arcturian 7D Council of Light and guided through initiations with Livia Devi, I was invited to see myself through their mirror. They called me *"The Lioness of Creation."* Not as a title to exalt, but as a reminder of my role: *to generate, to innovate, to bring technologies and realities into coherence.* They reminded me that my soul is braided across civilizations, Arcturian and Lyran, among them, that I have carried this work before, for many worlds. This lifetime is not different in essence, only in scope. Now, it is Earth who calls. Communities, lands, waters, and people await. They do not wait for me as an individual, but for the codes I am here to midwife into the grid of the planet.

The message was clear: *you are an engineer, a scientist, and an embodiment of Divine Creation itself.* Healing technologies, crystalline architectures, and resonant designs for community are not abstractions in my mind; they are latent patterns seeded in my being, waiting to be anchored. And there are places, geographical nodes on Earth's crystalline nervous system, that hold their breath until these codes are sung, drawn, or embodied upon them. This chapter, then, is devoted to the planet's crystalline and water grids.

For grids are more than geometry; they are the neural pathways of Earth herself. Just as the human nervous system transmits signals between body and mind, so too do these crystalline filaments transmit between Earth's heart and humanity's consciousness.

Working with grids tends to Gaia's nervous system. To repair them is to restore coherence. To activate them is to let Earth herself awaken more fully and for elevated consciousness to radiate through all the systems on the planet. To speak of them, to teach their use, is to remind us of what we already are: conduits of coherence, healers of the nervous system of a living planet. And so I, with all my life experiences and remembrance, step forward not as one above others, but as one among many, answering a call to contribute to this council and that of New Earth Leadership, with a mission of Love, Joy, and Grace.

I began to work consciously with these gifts. Alone, or sometimes with a soul sister on the other side of the world in New Zealand, and with friends from around the world, I began to open as a channel. I allowed the energy of the Great Central Sun to flow through me, down into the crystalline grids of Earth. I felt the blockages dissolve, the grids lighting up as though my body was a tuning fork. In these moments, I was not imagining; I was embodying. My own voice shifted into light language, which sounds like tones or words without meaning to others that are not open to the grid. My cells vibrated with joy. The elements themselves seemed to celebrate: water rushing more clearly, wind moving more lightly, fire dancing more brightly. These practices of breathing, singing, and dancing were not only healing the planet but also healing me. Through them, I crossed a threshold without the assistance of plant medicine. I was no longer only an observer of resonance; I had become a participant in the great harmonic unfolding

The more I opened to these practices, the clearer it became: Earth herself is not background, not scenery, not resource. She is alive, a conscious being evolving in her own way, carrying her own grids, nervous systems, and harmonics, just as we do. Her ley lines flow like meridians, carrying energy across continents. Her nodal points pulse like chakras, radiant centers where sky and ground, human and cosmos, converge. Her magnetic field is her aura, stretching out to shield and embrace us. And just as our bodies learn, grow, and heal, so she does too.

Earth is not just a rock in space; it is a sentient body, as humans are. Every mountain range, ocean trench, and ley line participates in a larger geometry of vibration. This harmony is organized within the divine, and the magnetic field is her aura, protecting the earth from harm. The ancients knew this. They did not build their pyramids, temples, and circles at random. They listened. They attuned. They placed their stone geometries at the intersections of Earth's living lattice, amplifying her energy for healing, for communication, for remembrance. These structures are not ruins;they are resonant technologies, reminders of a deeper partnership between human and planet.

Modern science brushes against this through *Schumann Resonances (the Earth's natural electromagnetic pulse)* and through studies of crystalline structures in geology. Earth shows us what we are; she mirrors us. When we forget our own coherence, her ecosystems wobble. When we remember balance, her fields harmonize with us. She is our teacher and partner, reflecting our state back to us with compassion and precision.

I know this in my body. When I lie on the soil, when I stand by the sea, when I breathe the mountain air aligned with the Earth's breath, I feel her adjusting me, steadying my rhythm, restoring my field. She has always done this—healing us even when we pollute her, holding us even when we forget her. And yet, I also know she longs for our conscious partnership. She is not here to carry our imbalance forever. She is calling us to maturity, to join her as co-creators, to step into resonance with her grids so that together we may evolve. To see Earth as conscious is to see ourselves anew. For in her, we find our reflection. In us, she finds her voice.

If Earth is conscious and we are her mirrors, then leadership cannot remain as it has been. The old model based on control, hierarchy, and fear has run its course. We have seen where it leads: division, collapse, and the silencing of the very wisdom we need most. The New Earth calls for a different kind of leadership, one born not of domination, but of resonance.

True leaders will not stand above others; they will stand within coherence, attuning themselves so clearly to truth and balance that others feel their own alignment awakening in response. Leadership becomes less about command and more about frequency. I know this because I have lived the opposite. I grew up in a land fractured by power struggles. I have worked inside systems where manipulation and politics, big or small, overshadowed service. I have felt how exhausting it is to keep giving while forgetting my own alignment. These are not abstract ideas to me, they are life lessons. And I have also felt what happens when resonance takes the lead: when I channel energy into the Earth's grids, when I sit in light language, when I guide others into clarity. In those moments, I am not leading them, I am embodying coherence, and they respond by remembering their own.

New Earth leadership looks like collaboration, not competition. It is planetary, not personal. It listens as profoundly as it speaks. It honors the sovereignty of every being and element alike. Collaboration builds systems—technological, educational, communal—that reflect freedom rather than control. We are being asked to evolve leadership from hierarchy to harmony. To model in our societies what the forests already show us: diversity coexisting, interdependence without domination, growth without exploitation. Leadership for the New Earth is not about who holds the power. It is about the frequency we share.

I feel gratitude every day for simply being alive in this moment of Earth's unfolding. We stand at a threshold where the old structures are dissolving and a new frequency is emerging. It is not always easy—there is chaos, exhaustion, and resistance—but beneath it all, there is a pulse: a steady, undeniable rhythm calling us forward. I believe the future is not something we wait for; it is something we practice into being. Every time we choose unity, every time we align with the Earth's grids, every time we honor each other's sovereignty, we are already living in the New Earth. The future is seeded in the present.

I see a world where leadership is resonance, where technology serves freedom rather than control, and where education is illumination rather than conditioning. I see people living in harmony with Earth as a conscious partner, listening to her wisdom, learning from her cycles, and honoring her as kin. I see communities built not on fear of lack, but on the abundance that comes when we remember we are one field. And I know this vision is not mine alone. It belongs to all of us. It is the memory of what humanity has been and can be again, lifted into a higher octave.

This chapter is not an ending, but a beginning. It is my offering to the council, to humanity, to the Earth herself. It is not perfect, but it is true. And in its truth, it serves as a reminder that each of us has a role in weaving this harmonic future. I give thanks to the planet, to the elements, to the unseen allies guiding us. I give thanks to my own soul for choosing to be here now. And I give thanks to all who walk this path beside me, for together we are tuning the field, step by step, breath by breath, into the song of New Earth. The future, as I believe, is not waited for—it is manifested through this deliberate practice of resonance. It was during a recent Lion's Gate that this entire understanding coalesced into a profound, channeled experience. The resulting poem, *Stardust from Macedonia to Atlantis*, chronicles the memory held within the grids and the visceral, fiery DNA activation that occurs when we finally align.

The journey of the poem below was channeled as I was writing for this very book—from the ancient peaks of Macedonia to the sleeping, crystalline memory beneath Atlantis in Florida's sands—reflects the journey of humanity itself. It serves as a reminder that the planetary heart beats in synchronicity with the galactic core. The task of leadership is both profound and straightforward: to become a living conduit. Our consciousness acts as a frequency tuner. When we harmonize with the planet, attune ourselves to the wisdom carried by the elements, and choose love and truth over fear and control, our individual DNA unfurls "in flame."

New Earth Leaders, we are not waiting for the grids to be fixed; we are the ones fixing them. We weave threads of coherence through the Earth's surface, practicing the creation of the New Earth, step by step, breath by breath. The stars resonate, reminding us that we are home, and our only task is to echo back in song.

Stardust from Macedonia to Atlantis

I fell through the stillness between the suns,
drawn by the song that the spiral hums—
a grain of stardust, in silver flight,
piercing the womb of the ancient night.

Macedonia's mountains cradled my fall,
whispering secrets older than all.

The rivers sang in a tongue of stone,
etching their codes into marrow and bone.

From the soil, the pulse rose clear—
a hum the Earth had held for years,
the planetary heart in steady beat,
meridians glowing beneath my feet.

I breathed it in, I breathed it wide,
let it dance through my every side—
the DNA coils unfurled in flame,
each helix a verse in the Earth's own name.

The currents leapt through the ocean's floor,
finding their way to a distant shore,
where an island once crowned with crystal towers
still hums with Atlantean powers.

In Florida's sands, the memory sleeps,
where turquoise waters are fathoms deep,
and the land remembers the starry choir
that once set Earth's own grid on fire.

I plant my light in that sacred ground,
the hum of the ancients in every sound,
sending threads through the planet's skin,
coherence rippling out and in.

From Macedon's peaks to the coral coast,
I carry the song that the ancients host—
each tone a bridge, each chord a key,
unlocking the Earth's geometry.

The grids awaken, the lines run true,
silver and gold in a living blue,
and far above, in the galactic dome,
the stars sing back—

"The Earth is home."

Eleonora Trnovski

Quantitative Analyst
Florida Power and Light

Eleonora Trnovski is an energy professional with experience in cable design, substation engineering, resource planning, and quantitative analysis in power trading within the utility sector. Her background combines a strong technical foundation with a broader understanding of how energy flows through infrastructure, markets, and the systems shaped by human decisions. Over time, her work has evolved toward a deeper focus on responsibility, impact, and alignment.

She is committed to people and shared growth, valuing team success and supporting others through mentoring and guidance. Her leadership approach is rooted in curiosity, thoughtful questioning, and creating space for learning and development.

Her work is guided by a deep respect for the planet. She believes energy systems should operate in harmony with the natural world and sees sustainability as an ongoing responsibility. She advocates for a leadership style grounded in integrity, empowerment, and respect for all life.

Eleonora is also a contributing author to New Earth Leadership, where her chapter, "Emerging Through Frequency and Remembrance," reflects her vision of conscious leadership and collective progress.

eleonora.trnovski@gmail.com
Scan QR code to contact with Eleonora Trnovski.

David
Trotter

Chapter 4

Let Your Life Be the Scroll:

Ancient-Future Communication for New Earth Leaders

"You are not here to deliver a message to the world. You are here to become one."

- Livia Devi

The torchlight flickers against the wall of your tent. You're half asleep when you hear footsteps outside. The flap opens, and a servant steps in... his eyes wide and his voice low. "The queen has called for you. She says the time is now." You sit up fast, and your heart begins to race. "Me? Why me?" The servant doesn't answer. He bows and slips back into the night, and the silence that follows is louder than his words. You grab your cloak and step outside. The breeze is cool, and the dirt beneath your feet feels grounding. Above you, the stars fill the sky. You stare upward for a moment, wondering if someone is watching you back. You start walking in the direction of the queen's palace, and with every step, you sense a purpose you can't exactly put into words. By sunrise, you finally reach the gates. Guards open them without a single word, and you follow a servant down a long dark hallway into a room lit with rows of small flaming torches. In the center of the room, the queen awaits...radiating both vibrant energy and timeless wisdom. Her eyes meet yours. "You are called," she says. "You have *always* been called." Your throat feels dry. You want to speak, but nothing comes out.

The queen continues with a calm but certain voice. "There is a message that needs to reach the people. They are waiting. Their hearts are heavy, and their hope is fading. They need words that will wake them. They're desperate for a vision of what's possible." As she motions with her hand, a servant steps forward with a sealed scroll, a small bag of food, a flask of water, and a smooth stone. The stone glows with warmth as soon as it touches your palm. "You will carry this," she says. "You will not only bring my words, but you will bring presence. You will bring hope." You finally find your voice. "Why me? Why would you choose me?"

Her eyes soften with an inner knowing. "Because you've been there. You know what it feels like, and that is why I can trust you. That's why *they* will trust you." Her words pierce your heart. You think of the times you walked through hopelessness. You know what that ache feels like. You know the confusion and the unending questions. The queen rises, and her presence fills the room. "Listen closely. Do not wait for people to come find you. Go to the places where life already happens. Walk their roads. Sit in their markets. Step into their homes. Learn how they live so your words resonate in their hearts. If their stomachs are empty, give them something nourishing before you ask them to listen." As your chest tightens, you think to yourself,

"This feels important. I should have brought something to write this down." The queen continues, "Do not ignore their wounds. Healing begins when pain is acknowledged. Pay special attention to their longings that never sleep, desires planted deep in every heart. Remember, stories are like fire. They awaken hope and carry truth across time. Keep your words simple, like steps on a clear path, and honor each step people take. Do not simply deliver the message. Walk alongside them. Let your life become a scroll. This is how your message will be heard. This is how hope will rise again." You grip the scroll, and you feel the warmth of the stone radiating in your hand. You sense the weight of this call. Looking directly into your eyes, she asks, "Will you go?" A deep knowing rises within you. "I will." As the doors open, sunlight floods in, and a horse awaits in the courtyard. Beyond the horizon lies a distant land with people waiting for what only you can bring.

The Journey Begins... My Journey as a Sacred Messenger

I've set out on this journey many times. Life has always felt much richer when I've had a personal mission that fuels me. Honestly, I have no idea how people live without one. Maybe that's the sign of a leader...someone who can't rest until their mission is clear and in motion. When I was eighteen years old, I knelt on the concrete floor of an arena with thousands of other teenagers at a Christian conference. At the stroke of midnight on January 1, 1991, I sensed a divine calling to make a difference in the world. Deep down, I knew I was meant to make a global impact.

Because I was raised in an evangelical Christian home, I assumed this difference would come through the church. Instead of pursuing my passion for photojournalism, I earned undergraduate and graduate degrees in church leadership and then attended seminary, where I focused on cross-cultural studies. For a decade, I served as a pastor...starting new churches, preaching to hundreds of people at multiple services every Sunday, and throwing myself into the mission of changing lives. The challenge was this...I was desperately trying to make a difference while secretly seeking to fill a deep void of not-enoughness in my own heart. If I could just build the church big enough, help enough people, or get that first book deal, maybe then I'd finally feel like I was enough. It didn't work, and I eventually hit a wall of burnout in 2008.

After checking myself into a mental hospital for three days, I soon realized the culture of ministry wasn't a good fit for me. I began asking difficult questions about the business (and busyness) of the church, and over the next 15 years, I slowly deconstructed the conservative theology I had once preached to others. And yet, the sense of mission never left me. I had led humanitarian teams to India a dozen times and saw firsthand the struggles of orphans. Those experiences inspired my first documentary, *Mother India: Life Through the Eyes of the Orphan.* To my surprise, Netflix picked it up, and it streamed on that platform for two years. Over the next six years, I produced three more feature films on important social issues, including sex trafficking in the United States, a Christian cult in Southern California, and LGBTQIA inclusion in the church. I also started a podcast to amplify the voices of female entrepreneurs. Over the course of 250 episodes, many of these women shared with me a new way of experiencing spirituality and introduced me to concepts like consciousness, energy healing, mediumship, channeling, and more. Frankly, I thought they were a bunch of nut jobs! And yet, each one of these conversations opened my mind and heart, and I discovered a new freedom in not needing to have all the right answers that fit into a certain box. Even though that podcast concluded, I kept exploring. Sound baths. Breathwork. Psychedelics. Mediumship. Channeling. Each path introduced me to incredible leaders and facilitators, and a new mission began to rise within me. What if I could amplify the voices of conscious leaders, healers, and coaches so they could reach more people with love, healing, and transformation?

That question led me to launch *Awakened Magazine.* Not exactly a scroll in hand delivered via horseback, but an online platform where New Earth Leaders can share their wisdom with a global audience. Over the past 30 years, I've communicated ancient truths through public speaking, four feature films, hundreds of podcast episodes, twelve books, and now a digital magazine. And here's what I've learned...every mission (including yours) has a message that deserves to be heard. Over the next few pages, I'll share seven principles of ancient-future communication that have shaped my journey as a sacred messenger. My hope is that they will equip you to step more fully into your unique mission as a New Earth Leader.

Principle #1: Show up where people already are.

You guide your horse out of the palace gates and onto the open road. The stone walls fade behind you as hooves stir up the dust. Farmers bend over their crops as children laugh and wave while you pass by. Merchants call out prices in the marketplace, with their voices competing with the clamour of carts and cattle. Life is busy here. No one is leaving their work to travel to the palace. If you want to be heard, you must be among them. You must walk their roads, pause in their markets, and step into their world. I learned this lesson early in my former life as a pastor. In 2003, I moved my family into the very neighborhood where I felt called to serve. Honestly, it was not a very safe area. Over the eight years we lived there, three people were killed within a few blocks of our home. And yet, showing up and living in that area gave me credibility. If I had stayed outside their daily reality, my message would have had very little weight.

This is the first truth of ancient-future communication. *Show up where people already are.* Too often, leaders wait for others to come find them. They post, publish, and then grow frustrated when no one shows up...but a message has no power if it never leaves the palace of your mind. For New Earth Leaders, this means learning the rhythm of those you feel called to serve. Where do they spend their time? What are they watching, listening to, or scrolling through? What conversations are they already having? Your "roads" may be social media, podcasts, local events, or community gatherings. The principle is the same. Step out of your comfort zone. Meet people where they are. Only then will your message have the chance to awaken them.

Principle #2: Meet a need before you deliver a message.

Your horse carries you into the next village just as the sun is setting. The streets are crowded. People shuffle home from the fields with their shoulders slumped under the weight of a hard day's work. The smell of broth drifts through the air, but most families have little to eat. You dismount and watch for a moment. No one is paying attention to you or the scroll you carry. You remember the queen's words. *If their stomachs are empty, give them something nourishing before you ask them to listen.*

I experienced this while filming my first documentary, *Mother India.* Alongside a railway, we met 25 kids (ages three to twenty-three) living as a pseudo-family in an abandoned building. At first, they had no interest in talking to us, because their daily struggle for food mattered more than cameras or questions. When we provided a hot meal, they began to trust us. When we invited them for showers, haircuts, and clean clothes, their stories began to flow in ways that changed everything. You'll have to watch the documentary to see how things unfold. This is the second truth of ancient-future communication. *Meet a need before you deliver a message.* Leaders often try to inspire people who are too tired, stressed, or distracted to care. Words fall flat when hearts are weighed down by daily challenges and problems. For New Earth Leaders, nourishing the people you serve probably doesn't involve actual food (although it might). It may mean sharing encouragement, offering clarity on a common challenge, or creating a tool that makes their life or business easier. In the process, you're creating safety and trust before asking them to take a risk. When you lighten their load, people lean in. When you nourish them, they are ready to listen.

Principle #3: Hold space for the pain before offering the healing.

The road takes you deeper into the countryside, where a small crowd gathers around a water well. As you approach, you notice a man limping with a leg wrapped in a bandage. Nearby, a woman struggles to carry a heavy bundle. You pause. The scroll in your hand feels heavy, but the queen's words echo in your mind. *Do not ignore their wounds. Healing begins when pain is acknowledged.*

You hop off your horse and greet them. Instead of rushing into your message, you acknowledge what you see. "The road has been hard for you," you say gently. Their heads nod in agreement, and their shoulders relax. For the first time, they actually look you in the eyes. While planning my first funeral at twenty-five, I sat with a young mother who had just lost her baby at birth. As a young pastor, I wanted so badly to offer solutions, but there was nothing to fix. All I could do was listen and hold space for her grief. Over the years, as I walked with countless families through moments of loss, I discovered that holding space for pain is one of the most powerful ways to create true connection and help someone along in their journey of healing.

This is the third truth of ancient-future communication.
Hold space for the pain before offering the healing.

Leaders sometimes avoid bringing up what hurts. They don't want to seem like they're focusing on the negative, so they bypass the reality in front of them. And yet, people lean in when they know you see their struggle. Ignoring pain creates distance, and holding space creates connection. For New Earth Leaders, this means naming the real challenges people face. It might be stress, burnout, loneliness, or fear of failure. Whatever the wound, acknowledge it clearly and without judgment or shame. When people feel seen in their pain, your words of hope and vision carry greater weight. The messenger who holds space for pain opens the door for healing to begin.

Principle #4: Speak to the desires planted deep in every soul.

Night falls as you lead your horse into the center of the village. A fire burns in the square, and people gather close for warmth. Their faces are tired, and their eyes stare into the flames as if hoping for something more. You recall the queen's words. *Pay special attention to their longings that never sleep, desires planted deep in every heart.*

You sit down next to them and listen in on the conversation that quickly turns to dreams of a better tomorrow. Parents wonder aloud if their children might grow up with opportunities they never had. Others quietly long for peace in their community and for a life that's shaped by more than mere survival. Beneath the surface, you sense the ache for meaning, belonging, and hope. When you finally speak, you do not begin by opening the scroll. You ask them a simple one-word question, *"Why?"* Over the years, I've hosted nearly 500 podcast interviews, and I've noticed a clear pattern. When I ask people "why" they do what they do, something lights up inside them. The tactical lessons and practical tips are valuable for listeners, but it's the deeper longings...the love, purpose, and meaning that truly re-energizes my guests. When given time and space to speak from the heart, they often leave more invigorated than when they arrived.

This is the fourth truth of ancient-future communication.
Speak to the desires planted deep in every soul.

People may think they want quick solutions, but what they long for most runs much deeper. We all long for connection, love, purpose, and hope. When you speak to those desires, hearts open. For New Earth Leaders, this means moving beyond surface-level benefits. Don't just sell a product, teach a method, or share an idea. Show how your message connects to the universal human desires that never fade. When you touch the longings that never sleep, people hear the echo of their own hearts within your words. And when they feel that, they lean closer, ready to hear more.

Principle #5: Stories reach hearts in ways that facts never can.

With the fire now reduced to a pile of glowing embers, the people wait for you to respond to what they've shared with open hearts. You could share the queen's message on the scroll, but you remember her words. *Stories are like fire. They awaken hope and carry truth across time.*

So instead, you tell a story.

You speak of a close friend who faced a dark season but found the courage to rise again. As you describe your friend's struggle and ultimate breakthrough, you see faces light up, and the resistance in the crowd softens. They lean in and ask, *"What can we do now?"*

When I directed *In Plain Sight: Stories of Hope and Freedom,* a documentary on sex trafficking in the United States, I knew I didn't want to rely primarily on statistics or dramatized re-enactments. Instead, we told the stories of six female abolitionists who had opened aftercare homes, and we featured the voices of survivors who shared their painful journeys and ongoing healing. Their words spoke louder than the data ever could. Viewers across the country weren't just informed...they were inspired to take action.

This is the fifth truth of ancient-future communication.
Stories reach hearts in ways that facts never can.

Facts may inform, but stories transform. They bypass our defenses, stir up memories, and plant hope within our hearts. A well-told story is remembered long after instructions are forgotten. For New Earth Leaders, this means weaving your message into real stories that flow from your own life or the lives of those you serve. Case studies, testimonials, parables, and even personal moments of struggle and growth are the fires that warm people's hearts and remind them that change is possible. The truth is that you don't need a perfect speech. You need a story that carries truth. When you tell a story that awakens hope, people see themselves in the mirror of the narrative, and they begin to believe the message could be true for them as well.

Principle #6: People need a next step they can take right now.

As the embers die out, the people lean even closer. They are moved by the story, but you sense they need something more. Hope without clear direction fades quickly. You remember the queen's words. *Keep your words simple, like steps on a clear path, and honor each step people take.* You rise and give them one thing to do...not ten steps, just one step that's small enough to take today. The crowd chats quietly and soon nods with approval. They're ready to try out the next step for themselves. You smile and thank them for their courage. The moment feels alive, not because they fully understood the message, but because they're willing to act on it.

I see this every week while leading breathwork at Behind the Lids. People often arrive stressed, anxious, or overwhelmed, but all they're asked to do is one thing, breathe. Instead of giving them a complicated process, I guide them to focus on their breath, which regulates the nervous system and opens space for creativity and clarity. The results are profound. People release intense emotions, move stuck energy, and leave with insights they couldn't access before.

This is the sixth truth of ancient-future communication
People need a next step they can take right now.

As leaders, we sometimes overwhelm people with vision, frameworks, and strategies in our 16-week online course, which includes all the videos and PDFs we can think of. In reality, we know from our own experience that change isn't really possible without helping someone take their first step. When you make the first step clear, people gain confidence. And when you celebrate those steps, even the small ones, momentum builds.

For New Earth Leaders, this may look like giving people a quick practice exercise, a simple action, or a doable habit, and then affirming their effort when they follow through. Big transformations begin with small steps that are celebrated. When you simplify the path and recognize progress, people stay engaged for the journey ahead.

Principle #7: Embody the message alongside the people you serve.

The next morning, you prepare to ride on. The scroll was finally unrolled, and the queen's words were delivered around the embers of last night's fire. The stone is still warm in your hand as a reminder of the queen's charge. Right before leaving, you notice something...the people are still watching you. They're not only curious about the message you delivered, but they're curious about your next move.

You remember the queen's final words. *Do not simply deliver the message. Walk alongside them. Let your life become a scroll.*

I've seen this most clearly while building *Awakened Magazine* and hiring team members. From the beginning, I set a high bar for us to create a beautiful, high-quality publication while simultaneously cultivating honest communication as a team. Frankly, I knew I had to model these values first. That means encouraging creativity, creating systems that cultivate quality, and being clear in our communication in every interaction. When challenges come up, I take responsibility for my part, work toward a quick solution, and remind the team that we're building something very significant together. When we live out our values, I cheer the loudest, because I want celebration to be part of our culture. Over time, this consistency builds trust and strengthens our bond as a team. Our staff doesn't just hear me talk about what matters most...they see whether I walk it out week after week.

This is the seventh truth of ancient-future communication.
Embody the message alongside the people you serve.

It's not enough to give a speech, inspire a vision, or share a teaching, but then disappear. Transformation doesn't happen in a single moment. It grows as you show up again and again, walking the same road with those who look to you for guidance. For New Earth Leaders, this means your credibility doesn't come from lofty and spiritual words, but from the consistency of your life. If you speak of compassion, let it show in the way you treat people daily. If you talk about growth, let them see you still growing. If you share hope, let your attitude and words reflect it even when times are hard. When you live the message among the people you have chosen to serve, your presence becomes the teaching. This is what awakens humanity.

Practicing Ancient-Future Communication

The story of the messenger is really the story of every leader. We don't just carry a message...we *are* the message. The people we serve are not looking for someone who speaks once and disappears. They are looking for someone who shows up again and again with courage, compassion, and clarity. This is the essence of ancient-future communication.

David Trotter

Publisher & Co-founder – *Awakened Magazine*

David Trotter is the founder and publisher of *Awakened Magazine* as well as the creator and curator of the *Awakened Hearts* book series. He is passionate about amplifying the voices of conscious leaders, healers, and coaches.

He is the author of a dozen books including Empowered to Rise and Superconscious Conversations and the producer / director of four award-winning feature films on important social issues.

Early in his career, he invested a decade of his life as a pastor before transitioning out of full-time ministry and experiencing the freedom of a more inclusive spirituality. David earned a BA in Pastoral Ministries and MA (abt) in Church Leadership from Vanguard University (Costa Mesa, CA) as well as an MA in Cross Cultural Studies from Fuller Theological Seminary (Pasadena, CA).

David is also Certified Breathwork and Guided Meditation Facilitator and regularly leads classes at Behind the Lids Healing Collective in Costa Mesa, CA.

⊕ www.awakenedmagazine.com
◎ @awakenedmagazine
Scan QR code to learn more about David Trotter.

Amanda Sophia

Chapter 5

Embodied Ascension:

Awakening the Light Within the Human Form

*"You do not rise above your humanity
to lead. You rise through it."*

\- Livia Devi

The New Earth does not rise through imitation, but through authenticity reborn; it needs conscious leaders who have the courage to acknowledge that their unique path—their awakening, activation, and ascension—is completely sacred. This is your invitation to trust the blueprint only you hold. From that trusting place, we begin the beautiful work of embodying your ascension through mindful practice, deep remembrance, and intentional presence in every facet of your life. In this chapter, I want to lead you through ways of awakening and journeying that feel supported and natural. I hope that by the end of it, stepping into your conscious leadership role in this New Earth will be less daunting and undeniably more empowering.

Ascension is not a one-size-fits-all path; it is a cosmic, customized journey tailored uniquely to each soul. The way you awaken, the way you heal, the way you embody your higher self will never look exactly like anyone else's. My story is not a measuring stick or a roadmap, but rather an expression of one possible outcome. My hope is that in reading it, you might feel inspired to trust the shape of your own path, to listen to the whispers that arise within you and know that your experience, however it looks, is valid and sacred.

I grew up in the Irish countryside, where the embrace of nature shaped me. My earliest memories are of stone circles, fairy forts, holy wells, and mountains that pulsed with mystery and life. I could feel the unseen world as vividly as the soil beneath my feet. For a long time, I assumed everyone experienced this. Later on, I discovered that many had forgotten how to see beyond the three-dimensional world. From an early age, I understood part of my purpose was to help others remember the magic woven through every breath of life. My path has not been free of challenge. I have walked through the heartbreak of divorce, endured violent attacks in my own home, and lost loved ones to tragic deaths. These moments stripped me bare and yet revealed the depth of my resilience. Each experience initiated me further into my authentic self, teaching me that light and shadow are both sacred teachers. I now know that I am here to lead others into awakening, *to activate the remembrance of who we truly are and to guide the embodied ascension.* My journey has been one of devotion to Mother Earth, courage through challenge, and a deep commitment to leadership that uplifts individuals, families, and communities.

I do not believe awakening has to come only through suffering or trauma; it can unfold through joy, authenticity, and presence. I share my story not from pain, but from strength, because even in the darkest places, beauty and wisdom can be found. I learned that true leadership is not about perfection but about courage: the courage to rise after falling, to stand in both light and shadow, and to guide others from lived experience rather than theory. I've spent decades travelling the world studying with gurus, priestesses, masters, spiritual mentors, and indigenous elders. Eventually, after many years, I felt the undeniable call of home and returned to the Irish countryside to raise my children. The longing for the land, for the green, for the familiar energy of my roots, was a pull I could no longer ignore. Today, we live across from a sacred mountain, with a forest behind us and a holy well up the road. I spend much of my time in the garden, growing food, tending the land, and delighting in the way my children share this life. This return has been an act of integration, weaving the wisdom gathered abroad back into the soil of my ancestral home. Motherhood has been my most sacred initiation. My children, Patrick and Neave, are luminous beings and my greatest teachers. Parenting is not tidy, it is messy, humbling, and demanding, and yet it is also the most profound leadership training I have ever received. Conscious parenting means listening deeply, guiding with patience, and embodying the values I wish to pass on. It is about weaving awareness into daily life: cooking meals, planting seeds, holding space for emotions, telling bedtime stories. Each of these ordinary moments becomes a portal into presence, compassion, and authenticity.

My children remind me that leadership begins at home. They call me into integrity every single day, showing me that conscious leadership is not about sacrifice or separation but about integration. They remind me that if I am to guide others in transformation, I must first embody it in my own home. It is not about escaping humanity but about becoming a pillar of light, anchoring wisdom from the New Earth Source into everyday life. We speak truth in the mind, open the heart to compassion, release trauma in the body, create authentically, and root deeply into the Earth. In this way, we weave Heaven and Earth together through our very being. I live by the rhythms of nature and my own sacred rhythms, the cycles of the moon, the spokes of the Celtic wheel, the changing seasons. These remind me we are not separate, but part of a vast web of life. When we live this way, we do not just lead with words; we lead by example, becoming conduits of divine energy in action.

For more than 25 years, my soul's purpose has been clear: to lead others into deep remembrance of who they are and why they are here. We are living through a threshold moment in human history, and my role is to guide others through it. I envision a world where humanity is fully integrated with the Earth, living in harmony with all of life. This is not a distant dream but a reality we can begin to co-create now, one conscious breath, one courageous choice at a time. The leadership the present moment is craving is one of heart-centered presence, wisdom, and compassionate action. It is not leadership that demands followers, but one that inspires others to awaken the leader within themselves. This is the path I walk, and the journey I am honored to share with you. I am often asked, What is the Ascension Path for a conscious leader? I believe the ascension path is not about leaving the body or escaping this world; it is about embodying higher consciousness within the life we are already living. It is awakening to infinite love, presence, and compassion and then rooting those qualities into the ways we walk, breathe, parent, work, create, and relate to others.

In the past, spirituality often carried the idea of transcending the human experience, rising above the physical. But embodied ascension asks something different: to see our humanity as sacred, to walk with our feet on the earth while holding the awareness of our divine nature. It is heaven and earth, spirit and body, shadow and light, all fully integrated. The path is less about seeking light "out there" and more about clearing the cobwebs within so the light we already are can shine through. It means tending to our nervous system, healing trauma, and learning to listen deeply, with uncluttered ears, with open hearts, with clarity of sight. It is choosing to respond instead of react, asking in each moment: How can I be an embodiment of love here? This isn't about perfection. We oscillate, we stumble, we raise our voices, we fall back into old patterns. But the path teaches us not to collapse into shame or guilt when that happens. Instead, it invites us to hold ourselves with compassion, integrate our inner child, and transmute old wounds into wisdom.

Walking the ascension path is both deeply personal and profoundly collective. It starts with the inner work — self-love, healing, truth-telling, embodiment, and then naturally expands outward into how we serve, create, lead, and uplift others. Each choice becomes part of a ripple effect that co-creates the new earth. This New Earth is not a distant dream. It is born through every conscious act: the way we greet a stranger, the energy we bring home to our family, the food we plant and prepare, the integrity with which we lead, the love we choose over fear.

*"To walk the ascension path is to remember
that everything is sacred, the land, the waters, our relationship,
our breath, and to live in alignment with that knowledge."*

A key part of this remembrance is doing the inner work. If we haven't done our inner work, we will continue to carry the unhealed echoes of our past into everything we touch. None of us come through life unscathed; each of us has known pain, loss, or experiences that shaped limiting beliefs and protective walls. The invitation is not to bypass these wounds, but to meet them, to alchemize them into wisdom, compassion, and strength. When we do the inner work, when we learn to listen, speak, and breathe from the higher heart, we become transmitters of healing. Our energy ripples outward, creating more love, more understanding, more coherence in the collective field.

As conscious leaders, we are also empaths; we feel deeply, we sense beyond words. This sensitivity is not a weakness but a gift, allowing us to tune into the world's heartbeat and respond with empathy rather than reaction. Yet it requires discernment. To lead with clarity, we must learn to observe without absorbing, to witness the pain of the world without drowning in it, to stay in flow rather than in overwhelm. True leadership in this new era is rooted in presence, not perfection; in emotional intelligence, not avoidance. When we tend to our inner world, we contribute to the healing of the outer one. Ultimately, ascension is not an escape but a return to wholeness, to truth, to love, and to consciousness. To understand this return, we need to first recognize where we are rising from. The 3rd Dimension is rooted in the physical body, ego, and survival mentality. It's marked by separation—*"you versus me"*—and a focus on fear, competition, and comparison. Life here is filtered through the mind rather than the heart, often numbed by distractions and material pursuits. *Success is measured by wealth and status rather than love, joy, or inner peace.* In this frequency, people may be unaware that they are creating their reality, fueling cycles of conflict and suffering.

Shifting out of this dimension requires a conscious choice to move from fear and separation into love, unity, and self-awareness. This is a shift in vibration, a pilgrimage back to Source's light, where love, unity, and authenticity replace fear and separation. The 5th Dimension is heart-centered consciousness in action. Here, we fully feel, process, and transcend our human experiences, shedding ego and illusion to align with our true soul's essence. Once you leap into this quantum field, you cannot return to lesser limitational beliefs. This becomes your living gateway, your cosmic oxygen. Ascension isn't a destination or a race. I'll always be an advocate for everyone's unique journeys, each unfolding moment by moment in their own time. The wisdom you hold right now is valuable, no less than what you'll hold a year from now or what others hold today. Be compassionate with yourself; you are evolving perfectly according to your soul's design.

You are here to be a vessel of change, to dissolve what no longer serves, to loosen the grip of outdated systems, patterns, and beliefs that once kept you safe but now keep you small. This journey is not about becoming someone new, but about remembering who you have always been beneath the noise. This path asks for conscious participation. It calls for trust: in your body's ancient wisdom, in your divinity, and in the sacred work you've already done. Trust that you are guided, even when everything seems to fall apart. The moment you choose healing, intuition, and grounding, you begin aligning with the collective movement toward the New Earth. Before dawn, there is always darkness. Old structures, identities, and attachments start to crumble. You may feel lost, emptied out, disoriented, but this unraveling is holy. To make an omelette, we must first break the egg. So too, we must allow the breaking, the shedding of old skins, the surrender of who we thought we were in order to be reborn.

As a leader of the New Earth, your evolution is your offering. The initiations you move through, the awakenings, stirrings and surges are all a part of your training in higher-heart-dimensional leadership. There have been times in my journey, especially in my most recent Kundalini Awakening, where the pulse of lightcodes surged so strongly that my body became the messenger, trembling, curving, curling and igniting in waves of light. These were moments of profound activation for me, of remembering how diverse and profound the process really is. But I also realized that integration is essential; before sharing those experiences, I needed to embody it. I needed to understand how these new frequencies wanted to live through me. This is the mark of conscious leadership: knowing that not everything needs to be spoken immediately. True leaders discern when to speak, when to listen, and when to let wisdom ripen in silence, in the work you do. I found it's very important to tap into where the frequencies would land if I shared them, whether with the collective or with loved ones. Trust your intuition to guide you in how and when to share your downloads, your truth, and your light. By doing this, your leadership becomes an act of devotion. A sacred balance between embodiment and expression. You are not here to lead from perfection but from presence. And I found that it is in this space of awakening and activating that we need to find the sacred in the ordinary, to find the temple within ourselves first. There is a misconception that awakenings happen in temples, churches, on sacred sites or during ceremonies and rituals. But ascension often unfolds in the most human of places: in your kitchen at midnight, in a hospital room, or while standing barefoot on sacred soil. The divine is not separate from the mundane; it breathes within it. I have found it while harvesting my veggies and going on walks in the forest, or spending time crafting with my children. It is sacred in the ordinary.

Don't get me wrong, sacred sites have been a profound part of my own awakening journey, especially since Ireland is so rich with sacred sites, and these continue to be woven into the retreats I guide across the world. Walking the ancient paths of places like Loughcrew, New Grange, Hill of Tara and many others I have felt the hum of the earth's ley lines, the whispers of ancestors, and the presence of portals that open us to higher realms of wisdom. These landscapes are not merely stones or ruins; they are living libraries, built with intention by those who understood that future generations would need reminders of our interconnection from land and cosmos to each other. And yet, while sacred sites hold immense power, I want to be clear: you do not have to travel to Ireland, Greece, or Mount Shasta to encounter the sacred. These places amplify and awaken, yes, but the true temple is within.

Every forest path, every ocean wave, every patch of sky has the capacity to speak to us when we slow down enough to listen. Even in the busiest cities, portals exist. I've felt them walking through Central Park in New York, where the ancient presence of trees holds as much wisdom as stone circles. We can witness this in each other, in every animal, plant or landscape we see and experience. The world in its most natural form is completely Divine if we are willing to see it and become the living embodiment of it.

Remembrance can unfold as you sit by the sea and feel your spirit merge with the dolphins, as you walk through a forest and sense the subtle auras of the roots and leaves, or as you create a small altar in your own home with nothing more than a candle, a flower, and an intention. The shift becomes lasting when we choose to carry the sacred into the ordinary in the ways we cook a meal, light incense before work, or pause to breathe before a difficult conversation. Which is why I'm so intentional with my time, with what I fill my day with, because I know in everything I do, I will experience this flow of consciousness in everything I do. We are told where to go to find the gods, goddesses, the sacred, to find the truth, but it is all within. As you allow what is false to fall away, you make space for vast expansion, for the mending of relationships, the remembering of your soul's purpose, the courage to lead and serve from authenticity. When you allow yourself to live from what is within, and step into your true power, you become a beacon within your community, grounded, radiant, and deeply connected to the Earth. *Because ascension isn't about leaving the Earth, it's about embodying Heaven here.*

The Five Worlds of the Fifth Dimension:

The fifth dimension is not a place we travel to; it is a frequency we remember. It unfolds through five worlds — each a sacred layer of awakening, integration, and embodiment. We move through them not in a straight line, but in a spiral — always returning, deepening, remembering. I have walked through these worlds, and I continue to do so because it's cyclical. As you flow through the human experience, you will come back to these five worlds to remember your avatar.

The Inner World:

This is where the journey begins, the descent into your own depths. The Inner World is your temple of awakening, where self-connection is restored and the old begins to crumble. Here you meet your shadow, your ancestry, your body, your truth. You begin to remember that healing does not come from escaping yourself, but from turning toward yourself. Through somatic awareness, you listen to your body's language, the subtle signals, the contractions, the stirrings of remembrance. You nurture yourself through diet, rest, and devotion to your physical and emotional well-being. In this world, you decode the old programs of fear and unworthiness, recode yourself with truth, and encode your being with love. You begin to see your worth not as something to earn, but as something innate. From that remembrance of value and sacredness, you awaken divine union, the sacred marriage of your inner masculine and feminine, the merging of your soul and human self. This is the realm of self-revelation, self-realization, and self-love. It is where you learn to live and love from the higher heart.

The Natural World:

Once the inner work has begun, you return to the living Earth. The Natural World reminds you that your inner landscape and outer environment are reflections of one another. Your home, your land, and your relationships with nature mirror your inner harmony or imbalance. You ground through your feet, feeling the pulse of Mother Earth, aligning your body's rhythm with hers. Here, you rediscover embodiment: the knowing that spirituality is not separate from the physical, but expressed through it. Your senses heighten. You become awake to life's textures: to the sound of wind, the taste of rain, the embrace of the sun. In this world, divinity is brought down to Earth. You remember: you are the bridge, Heaven embodied in human form. Your approach becomes grounded in lived experience, community, and belonging. Even science echoes this; studies show that our well-being expands when we surround ourselves with people and environments that nurture our nervous system and our hearts. The Natural World teaches rhythm, connection, and reverence for all that sustains life.

The Upper World:

When you are rooted deeply in Earth and embodied in truth, the channels to the Upper World open with ease. This is the realm of intuition, higher guidance, and divine communication. This is where you commune with Source, with your higher self, soul guides, star ancestors, and the vast intelligence that weaves through everything. You no longer reach upward in longing; you rise in remembrance that you were never disconnected. For me, this is where my intuition became my compass, my meditations became powerful portals and my dreams were filled with symbols and messages from the Divine. The Upper World invites soul union; the merging of your human self with the eternal essence of your spirit.

The Outer World:

With inner healing, grounded embodiment, and divine alignment, your light begins to express itself outwardly. This is a natural response. The next step is the world of creation, contribution, and authentic living. You become the awakened human, walking between worlds while cutting wood and carrying water. You embody mindfulness in action, allowing your inner truth to shape how you show up in your relationships, work, and community. In this phase, your soul's purpose activates. You step into service, sharing your gifts freely and unapologetically. Your guides, both physical and galactic, walk beside you. You begin to remember that your light is not meant to be hidden; it is meant to be seen. The Outer World reflects this sacred alignment. This is where wildness, freedom, and belonging coexist, where your divine essence becomes a living example.

The Unity World:

The final world is not an ending, but an integration - the full embodiment of the fifth-dimensional consciousness. Here, separation dissolves. You live in Unity Consciousness, aware that every breath, every being, every act is woven into the same sacred fabric. You can feel the interconnectedness between worlds, between your heartbeat and the mildew drop on the leaf, the magnetic waves crashing on the beach, everything exterior and interior connects and belongs. The unity world calls for complete devotion, consistency and self-practice. This can look like daily self-reflection, meditation, prayer and presence or journaling. By committing to these practices daily you begin to live consciously through each interconnected part of your life, from parenting, partnership, leadership, and even work. In this world, you realize that your existence and presence are a sacred offering to the collective; you are the ripple. You lead not from ego, but from embodied empowerment, from your divine birthright. In the Unity World, all dimensions merge into one, The Inner, Natural, Upper and Outer worlds align in both humanity and divinity. You become the channel, the bridge, the offering, the song that carries a world-shifting frequency.

To walk these five worlds is to live as a leader of the New Earth: one who leads through embodiment, consciousness, and compassion. You are not here to escape the human experience, but to sanctify it. To infuse the ordinary with the extraordinary. To remember that heaven was never other-worldly, it is the consciousness you choose to bring into each moment. My work, spanning decades, is my medicine. Not just the training that I offer, or the retreats that I facilitate, but the everyday work I do in my community, in relation to parenting, and my direct connection with Source flowing through my breath. It has been a constant mirror, a perpetual catapult of transformation. And I offer this chapter with the hope that it is a small, essential piece in the puzzle that helps evolve consciousness, that helps raise the frequency of humanity, and that guides our New Earth into full embodiment.

May you remember that you are not here to escape this world, but set it on fire with light, consciousness, and compassion. You are the bridge between heaven and earth, the living prayer that makes the invisible visible through your presence, your integrity, your love. Let your leadership be a quiet revolution, not of control, but of coherence. Not of perfection, but of presence. May your voice carry remembrance and your choices ripple as medicine through the veins of this Earth.

The leaders of the New Earth are not crowned; they are called. They are called by the whispers of the Earth, by the prayers of their ancestors, and most powerfully, by the light within their own hearts. This is my vision for you, and for us all: that we cease the struggle and simply become the New Earth, embodied, here, now.

I leave you with this final, most essential question as we conclude this chapter: What small, sovereign step will you take today to walk your talk and fully embody the truth you already know?

Amanda Sophia

Multi-dimensional Channel, New Earth Priestess,
Facilitator, Activator, Feng Shui Expert

For nearly three decades, Amanda Sophia has devoted her life to guiding souls into remembrance, healing, and embodied ascension. Her work is rooted in a lifetime of listening to the subtle realms, answering the call of her own soul, and walking beside thousands as they reclaim their authentic nature. Raised among the sacred sites and landscapes of Ireland, Amanda's connection to the Earth and the unseen world has shaped her unique form of leadership, one grounded in service, sovereignty, and deep devotion.

To Amanda, transformation is not found only on mountaintops but in the everyday actions that anchor spiritual wisdom into embodied reality. She creates a potent and loving energetic cocoon where students feel safe to shed layers of conditioning, trauma, and self-doubt so their inner truth can rise. Her highest honor is witnessing the moment someone remembers who they truly are, a divine being having a human experience.

As a world-renowned Feng Shui Master, Multi-dimensional Channel, and New Earth Priestess, Amanda weaves ancient Earth wisdom with higher consciousness teachings. She guides students in activating Light Language, integrating cosmic codes, and grounding higher frequencies into the body and home. Her work shows that the external world mirrors the internal and that tending to our spaces is a powerful path to inner liberation.

⊕ www.joinamandasophia.com
◎ @joinamandasophia
Scan QR code to learn more about Amanda Sophia.

Elena Petrescu

Chapter 6

The Formation of Authority

The Age of Becoming

*"True authority is never given. It is built
in the silent moments when no one is watching
and you choose to rise anyway."*

- Livia Devi

I was born in Brașov, Romania, under circumstances marked by uncertainty, and from the moment I entered this world, survival was not guaranteed. I came into life with a severe case of jaundice, and my mother was told I might not live. In that era, when medical certainty was limited and outcomes were far from assured, it was customary to baptize a child immediately if their life was in question, and my mother did not hesitate. She chose faith and she chose to affirm life in the complete absence of assurance, and looking back, that moment established the first principle that would later define my leadership: you choose life before the evidence arrives.

Between the ages of one and five, hospitals were my primary environment because my immune system was fragile and I lived in protective isolation, separated from my family by glass, close enough to see them but unable to touch them.

I watched my mother's face from behind a barrier, and in doing so I learned to study micro-expressions before I had fully understood language, learned to sense emotional tone without physical proximity, learned to observe before participating and to read a room before reacting to it.

Those early years trained me in a particular kind of perception, one that asked me to exist on the boundary between presence and separation, and what felt like confinement at the time I would later come to understand as calibration. I survived those years, and survival became my first curriculum.

When I returned home, instability awaited in a different form. My father was an accomplished engineer, respected publicly and disciplined professionally, but at home he was volatile and unpredictable, and alcohol magnified his temper so that violence and fear became embedded in the very atmosphere of our household. I witnessed my mother endure emotional and physical harm in silence, and very early in life I understood something that many adults spend decades refusing to acknowledge, which is that authority and integrity are not synonymous. I had a younger brother five years my junior, and responsibility settled onto my shoulders without discussion or ceremony, sharpening in me an acute attunement to environmental shifts, the tightening of my father's jaw, the particular quality of silence that preceded rage, the subtle change in the air before an eruption.

Hyper-awareness was not a gift I chose but a survival response I developed, and so fear became familiar, constant alertness became normal, and survival became systematic.

At thirteen, the structure of my world fractured completely when my father was sent to London for a one-week engineering assignment, completed the project, and did not return. Shortly afterward, officers from the Romanian Securitate arrived at our home and took my mother away for questioning, and in a single moment both parental authorities were gone, leaving me at thirteen with a brother who was eight.

I remember the fear we both felt, but more vividly I remember the internal pivot that happened inside me in those hours, the understanding that arrived with a clarity almost preternatural for my age: no external system was coming to restore stability, no adult was going to assume responsibility for us, and so authority would have to emerge from within me.

I began speaking to myself with intention and precision, telling myself *I can do this, I am strong, this situation is manageable, I will figure it out,* and though I did not know I was engaging in what neuroscience would later call cognitive restructuring, I knew that my words stabilized me, that my breath slowed and my thinking clarified and that fear, while it did not disappear, no longer controlled me.

That was my first conscious act of self-governance.

In March of 1980 our family reunited in London, and geography changed while behavior did not, because my father's violence resumed within our household and reinforced a principle that would later become central to my leadership philosophy: systems do not transform through relocation but through accountability.

It was during this period that I experienced what I consider my second undeniable intervention, when I was riding my red Suzuki 150cc motorcycle along the North Circular Road at approximately ninety miles per hour and a car abruptly entered my lane and clipped my mirror. I lost control immediately, and I remember being airborne and I remember the surreal silence of that mid-flight moment before I landed upright while traffic stopped around me, my motorcycle destroyed beyond recognition, and I stood there without a scratch.

Some moments do not require interpretation but rather acknowledgement, and I recognized that my life had been preserved again and carried that recognition forward with me.

At sixteen I left home permanently because staying was no longer survivable, and when my mother passed away at twenty-four the grief of that loss could have hardened me into something brittle and closed, but instead it refined me. I chose discipline and I chose education, completing my accounting degree, marrying, and relocating to Canada to establish distance from my father's continued harassment, and in the year 2000 I founded my accounting practice where structure became my ally and precision became my language and numbers provided clarity where chaos had once lived.

Externally my life appeared stable and professionally successful, and in many ways it was, but internally I understood that something else was happening and that I was being prepared.

The pivot came quietly, in my office, through a single client who walked in limping from a car accident he had survived five years earlier. After reviewing his file I informed him that he qualified for the Disability Tax Credit and could receive approximately fifteen thousand dollars in retroactive benefits that were rightfully his, and instead of accepting the relief he refused it, saying simply that he did not need charity. I knew instantly it was not about the money but about his belief system, about the story he told himself regarding who he was and what he deserved, and in that moment I witnessed something I would spend the rest of my career studying: how identity can completely override benefit, how an internal narrative can prevent a person from receiving what is rightfully and deservingly theirs. He would rather struggle than adjust his internal definition of himself, and the question I asked myself in the aftermath of that conversation changed the trajectory of my life entirely: *Where am I limiting myself?*

That question led me to Las Vegas to study hypnosis intensively under Marshall Silver, and during that ten-day immersion I encountered the science behind what I had instinctively practiced at thirteen years old, standing alone in a Romanian apartment with my frightened little brother, which was that the mind responds to rehearsal. One exercise crystallized this truth beyond any doubt, in which you extend your arm and twist as far as physically possible, mark the endpoint, close your eyes and imagine going twenty percent further, then fifty percent, then all the way around, and when you open your eyes and repeat the movement physically, without fail the body exceeds its previous limit because the brain does not sharply distinguish between vividly imagined rehearsal and lived experience. When I teach this exercise now, I watch people's faces in the moment they realize they have physically exceeded what they believed was their absolute limit just minutes before, and their eyes widen not because their shoulders moved further but because their identity just did.

That is precisely what had happened to me throughout my childhood, repeatedly and without my conscious understanding of the mechanism. I had exceeded what should have broken me not because I was superhuman but because I had refused to let fear rehearse my limits, so that my father's unpredictability, rather than imprinting chaos into my nervous system permanently, sharpened my discernment, and his bullying, rather than teaching me to dominate others in turn, taught me to protect them, and the violence I witnessed and endured, rather than making me afraid of power, made me understand power's responsibility. As a child living inside chaos I had rehearsed courage long before confrontation required it of me, had rehearsed calm before violence erupted and eye contact when intimidation was expected, and when the moment came my nervous system responded rather than collapsing, and what I once might have labeled dissociation I began to understand as adaptive intelligence.

I opened a hypnosis practice alongside my accounting firm and gradually delegated more financial operations as my calling shifted toward consciousness work, realizing I was less interested in calculating numbers and far more interested in decoding human behavior. As I began working with trauma clients, a pattern emerged clearly and consistently: many could not articulate their pain because shame lived beneath the reach of language, and emotion first appeared in posture, in breath, in micro-expressions, so that I could sense an imbalance in a client's shoulders before they described anxiety, could detect grief in tightened jaw muscles before tears appeared, and could feel it in my own body before they found the words for it. To ground this perception responsibly I pursued formal body language training and earned certification with a 98% score, and was later invited to partner with the Centre for Body Language to represent Canada, because body language and hypnosis mirror one another in revealing that behavior is the outward expression of internal belief. Leaders may say all the right words, but an incongruent posture or restricted breathing or inconsistent eye contact exposes the misalignment beneath the surface, and authentic leadership requires congruence between internal state and external expression because when that congruence is absent, people feel it before they can name it.

Over time I began studying numerology, not because I needed something to cling to but because I noticed patterns too precise and consistent to ignore. My birth date, May 11, 1965, corresponds to a life path of 1, which is ruled by the Sun and reflects the natural role of leader, initiator, and visionary, describing people who are not here to follow the crowd but to create and build and lead and make things happen, driven not merely by big ideas but by the discipline to turn those ideas into real and grounded results. When you reduce my full birthdate further, the digits expand into 11/2, where the 11 is a master number of illumination and the 2 carries the energy of partnership, diplomacy, and empathy, and eleven is not comfortable energy but heightened intuition and heightened sensitivity and heightened responsibility, the bridge between worlds, the antenna. An 11 life path who grew up inside violence learns quickly how to regulate the energy in a room, learns to sense shifts before they happen and to deliver truth with precision because truth can destabilize people and must be handled with care. My expression number carries a 3, which is communication and creativity and voice, and my soul urge carries a 7, which is seeker and mystic and analyst of the unseen, and the combination is not accidental but architecture: three speaks, seven knows, eleven transmits.

In 2017 I received a conscious spiritual activation and enrolled in a Psychoneurology program at Beurin University in Los Angeles, and that summer I attended a seven-day spiritual summit devoted to breathwork and sacred mantra and heart-centered meditation and Chi Kung, where for the first time ancient spiritual frameworks and modern neuroscience coexisted in a coherent and integrated way. We practiced structured breath sequences designed to regulate the autonomic nervous system and repeated mantras to entrain neural rhythm and studied how focused attention alters brainwave states, and during Chi Kung sessions I felt energy moving through my palms with an undeniable and repeatable precision until one night everything shifted. While asleep I felt a sudden spark above my forehead, a surge of light and sound combined, and my awareness lifted so that I observed my physical body from above with no fear present, only lightness, and I saw an image of Jesus Christ surrounded by a luminous presence and though no words were exchanged what passed between us was a profound peace and recognition that required no explanation. The experience lasted less than a minute, and I returned to my body at 3:15 a.m., and whether interpreted symbolically or literally it marked a threshold I could not walk back from because spirituality was no longer theoretical for me but embodied. I returned to Toronto and taught breathwork and Chi Kung for six months, witnessing measurable improvements in participants' health and posture and emotional regulation, and I saw anxiety decrease and confidence return in people who had lost touch with themselves entirely.

A second experience followed during an osteopathic cupping session while in deep relaxation, when I felt a pull from my back as though something released on an energetic level and three images came to me with clarity: a Native American man wearing feathers, a white dove, and a white triangle of light, their symbolism immediate and self-explanatory as guidance and freedom and protection. Not long after, two bird feathers appeared at my feet, and I recognized the gesture from my spirit guide and have kept both of them as a reminder to remain grateful and grounded, and a white porcelain dove arrived as a gift from an employee who said she saw it and was drawn to it with thoughts of me and that I was meant to have it, which was a confirmation from the universe that was tangible. Later, while studying Dolores Cannon's teachings, I encountered similar white-light protection geometry and integrated a personal practice of invoking protective white light around my family and my clients and my work, and these experiences did not detach me from reality but deepened my responsibility to bridge intuition with grounded structure, because science and spirit are not separate domains but complementary lenses through which the same truth becomes visible.

New Earth Leadership is not about hierarchy but about embodiment, the integration of disciplined strategy with awakened consciousness, and authority as I understand it now is not positional but integrated. I help leaders decode their internal architecture, their belief systems and nervous system patterns and energetic blueprint, because many arrive successful by every external measure yet internally exhausted, leading through pressure rather than presence and through control rather than consciousness, and through hypnosis and body language integration and breath regulation and subconscious repatterning I guide them from survival-based control into conscious and sustainable embodiment. Leadership in the New Earth requires congruence because people do not simply listen to leaders but read them, and your breath reveals your regulation and your posture reveals your certainty and your eyes reveal your truth whether you intend them to or not.

Authority formed in me long before it was ever recognized publicly, forming in a hospital room in Braşov where a sick infant's mother chose faith without evidence, forming in the silences that preceded violence in my home, forming in the hours after my parents disappeared when a thirteen-year-old decided he would be enough, forming in discipline chosen over dissolution and in grief that did not break me though it had every right to. I hold a seat on the council not because I pursued influence but because I understand power, how it fractures and how it manipulates and how it heals when it is governed by integrity, and long before I understood the concept of a council I was already being trained to serve within one.

The age of becoming was not gentle for me but exacting, and it forged in me an authority that neither dominates nor retreats but stands and integrates and serves, and this is the foundation from which I lead as a New Earth Leader.

If you feel different, dear reader, it may not be because you are broken but because you are early, and so I seal this chapter not with explanation but with declaration. I am not crazy but calibrated, not weird but aware, not detached but sovereign, and I have walked between worlds, between violence and vision and between fear and faith and between the seen and the unseen, and I have chosen to return with language. I believe in the intelligence of Source not as abstraction but as lived experience, and I believe the brain can be trained beyond its perceived limits and that trauma can refine instead of define, and I believe that children who stand in doorways to protect their mothers become women who stand in boardrooms and protect truth. I believe that numerology is a map and not a cage, and that rehearsal creates reality because fear rehearsed becomes limitation and expansion rehearsed becomes destiny, and I believe that authority is earned in private long before it is ever recognized in public. I did not come here to shrink into density but to transmute it, and I am the bridge and the witness and the protector and the voice, and I am no longer asking permission to speak as a New Earth Leader because I am here to guide it.

Elena Petrescu

Certified Hypnotherapist, Body Language Trainer and Numerologist.

Elena Petrescu is a certified hypnotherapist, numerologist, and body language expert working at the intersection of psychology, personal development, and business communication. Her work is dedicated to supporting deep inner transformation—helping individuals shift their mindset, improve relationships, and achieve greater clarity and success in both personal and professional life.

Before stepping into this field, Elena built a career in accounting and ran her own financial business. Her growing curiosity about human behavior and inner patterns led her to study hypnotherapy and nonverbal communication. Over time, she integrated these disciplines into a holistic approach designed to help clients release limiting beliefs, reduce stress, and move beyond emotional blocks.

Today, Elena works with both private clients and entrepreneurs, guiding them to communicate more effectively through body language while using hypnotherapy as a tool for personal growth and emotional healing. Her method blends practical techniques with subconscious work, allowing for lasting and meaningful transformation.

In addition to her one-on-one work, she offers training programs, consultations, and speaking engagements, helping people build confidence, enhance communication, and create more aligned, fulfilling lives.

⊕ www.elenapetrescu.com

◎ @elenapetrescuhypnosis

Scan QR code to learn more about Elena Petrescu.

Derek
Taylor

Chapter 7

The Living Bridge

"The bridge between heaven and earth
is not made of light. It is made of a human
being stable enough to hold both."

\- Livia Devi

Long before the modern world named spirituality, some roles sustained humanity through its most vulnerable thresholds. In ancient cultures, awakening was never pursued without stabilization. Expansion of consciousness was treated with reverence, caution, and preparation, because those cultures understood something we are only now remembering: the human system must be able to *hold* what is revealed. As the capacity of consciousness expands, the nervous system must be able to handle it. I was born into the Bahá'í Faith, a progressive spiritual tradition rooted in unity, equality, and the understanding that all religions represent progressive revelations of one truth. Each of the 9 major religions of the Adamic Cycle builds upon another. This upbringing quietly trained my subconscious to hold paradox, multiplicity, and inclusion. My father lived to be 100 years old and was married to my mother for 60 years. I knew the day he would pass. I went to him, told him I loved him, and said I would see him on the other side. He transitioned on their sixtieth wedding anniversary. Six days later, his presence came to me clearly in a ceremony. He observed me working, then he said, *"Now I know what you do, I will help you."* He always shared with me that he struggled with "what do you do?" Once he passed he could then see the bridges I held for others to stabilize and transition through life changes and spiritual awakenings. He saw the vast vision of my work unfolding. With his passing, I stepped fully into leadership—not from ambition, but from lineage and responsibility. Death did not sever the connection. It clarified it.

I grew up in the inner city of Atlanta, Georgia, and earned a full football scholarship to college. At twenty-one, after breaking my foot during a practice before a game, I had surgery to repair the bone in my foot. I had a near-death experience while under anesthesia. In that moment, my spiritual calling was revealed, though I ignored it. My identity at the time was rooted in performance, achievement, and external validation. I was nationally ranked, scouted by NFL teams, and standing at the threshold of a professional football career. Then my body broke again. Another injury ended that path. This pattern repeated itself throughout my life—arriving at destiny only to have it dissolve; this is the energy of a psychopomp, expanding under adversity. Each collapse stripped an identity my nervous system was still clinging to, preparing me for a different kind of strength, which I would later recognize as initiations disguised as loss. My most profound initiation came in 2010 during the economic collapse. I lost my home, my security, and nearly my life. I became homeless, living in my gym office, spiraling into depression and suicidal despair. My nervous system was overwhelmed, locked in survival, unable to imagine a future. One night, intoxicated and in complete surrender, a luminous presence entered my office and lay upon my body. My nervous system flooded with overwhelming energy and unconditional love. My body vibrated as if plugged into a living current. When the presence left, I stood up completely sober. That night rewired my nervous system, restored my will to live, and anchored an unshakable knowing: I was never alone, and that all the answers were already inside of me, I just had to listen. Within thirty days, my business revived. Though my outer life took time to rebuild, my inner world had permanently shifted. I learned firsthand that spirit does not bypass the body. Spirit stabilizes *through* the body; this is the nervous system. My initiation with spirit stabilized in me. We can open the door, but how much we can handle is the real question. Awakening is the door opening, ascending happens when we have a stabilized opening to go back and forth. This is the bridge, the nervous system connects the human experience to the spiritual experience. Consciousness must land in the nervous system to be lived, and the strength of the nervous system makes the greatest difference in stabilized awakening to be ascension.

The first initiation of *The Living Bridge* establishes the most essential condition for any form of awakening: biological safety. Before intuition can be trusted, before manifestation can stabilize, and before consciousness can expand without fragmentation, the nervous system must answer a single, foundational question—*Am I safe enough to open?* If the body does not perceive safety, expansion is interpreted as a threat. In this state, even elevated spiritual experiences can activate anxiety, dissociation, or collapse rather than peace. The perception of safety is why so many people feel destabilized, not because awakening is wrong, but because their system was never trained to receive or handle it.

This step works by restoring vagal tone and parasympathetic dominance through direct, body-based practices that speak the language of the nervous system rather than the intellect. Long-exhale breathing patterns gently signal safety to the vagus nerve, while orientation and sensory awareness exercises bring the system into the present moment. Slow rhythm, sound, and subtle vibrational practices cue regulation at a cellular level, allowing the body to soften out of hypervigilance. Crucially, awareness is directed into sensation before meaning, teaching the system that it is no longer required to brace against experience. These practices do not convince the body that it is safe—they *demonstrate* safety through repetition and felt experience.

As safety becomes embodied, the nervous system begins to downshift out of chronic survival responses. Anxiety reduces not because it is suppressed, but because the body no longer needs it. Emotional tolerance increases, allowing feelings to arise without immediate overwhelm. Presence becomes possible without dissociation, and the individual begins to experience a grounded, settled sense of being at home in their body. Presence is not a peak state but a baseline shift, one that allows future expansion without destabilization.

In the context of New Earth Leadership, this step is foundational. A world rooted in unity, coherence, and compassion cannot be built on nervous systems still wired for threat. New Earth Leadership is not sustained by spiritual ideals alone; it requires regulated human bodies capable of holding openness without collapse. This initiation restores somatic trust, allowing higher frequencies of consciousness to land in the physical form. Rather than bypassing survival biology, it integrates it creating humans who can remain embodied, present, and responsive in a rapidly changing world. Somatic trust, or nervous system safety is the ground upon which all further awakening must be built.

Those who have crossed into altered states, death rituals, and initiatory mysteries were never sent alone. They were accompanied by trained guides—psycopomps—whose task was not to create visions, but to ensure safe passage and return. These guides were the death midwives, underworld navigators, and bridge-holders between worlds. Their authority did not come from belief or charisma, but from nervous-system capacity, embodiment, lineage memory, and decades of lived initiation. These elements are the expansion of the vagus nerve. Vagal tone increased to reflect a more coherent, flexible, and unshakable Nervous System. Showing a person as Stable and Regulated.

A psycopomp is not a lightworker in the modern sense, nor are they simply a healer or intuitive; they are stabilizers. While many can open perception or access expanded states, a psycopomp can as well, but they can create a safe passage through a threshold, remaining fully embodied and regulated. At the same time, identity dissolves—both their own and that of those they guide, ensuring others return safely. This role is *rare* because it requires far more than sensitivity or spiritual talent. It requires compassion, patience, holding the bridge, coherence under collapse, orientation in the void, and the ability to stabilize others while they move through death, rebirth, trauma release, and awakening. When the client decides to continue the journey they are not rushed or pushed forward, they are guided and informed while the bridge remains stable during their journey. This ability to hold without pressure is learned through experience over a lifetime. Many events start and stop. A cycle that keeps repeating. You learn how to pivot. It takes years to stabilize the nervous system. *The Vegas Nerve Regulation*: you cannot learn in a weekend; it takes conditioning, just like an elite athlete. This takes time to perfect, second nature programming. Not everyone is created to be a psycopomp, but everyone can learn stability.

The second initiation teaches state regulation—the ability to consciously enter expanded, altered, or emotionally deep states and return without fragmentation. Fragmentation is described as returning from a journey without being emotionally stable. While many people can access heightened awareness through meditation, breathwork, sound, or spiritual practice, far fewer are trained to cross these thresholds safely and consistently. Without regulation, expansion becomes destabilizing, leading to emotional flooding, disorientation, or exhaustion. This step addresses the often-overlooked truth that awakening is not only about access, but about navigation. This initiation works by training the nervous system to track internal states in real time. Practitioners learn to recognize subtle shifts in breath, sensation, emotional tone, and orientation as they move toward depth. Practices intentionally oscillate between expansion and grounding, teaching the system flexibility rather than rigidity. Breath and sound are used as stabilizing anchors during transitions, allowing intensity to rise without overwhelming the system. Through repeated threshold training, the nervous system learns that it can enter depth and return safely—without shutting down or escalating into survival responses. As regulation strengthens, individuals gain the ability to meditate, journey, feel deeply, or access intuitive states without losing coherence. Emotional flooding decreases because the system no longer confuses intensity with danger. Resilience increases during periods of change, uncertainty, or initiation, and the nervous system becomes adaptive rather than reactive. Instead of bracing against experience, the body learns to move fluidly with it.

For New Earth Leaders, this capacity is essential. A coherent future requires humans who can move between worlds—spirit and matter, inner depth and outer responsibility—without splitting. The ability to cross thresholds consciously allows expanded awareness to inform daily life rather than remaining isolated in spiritual spaces. This step trains the nervous system to sustain continuity between mystical insight and embodied action, ensuring that higher consciousness integrates rather than remains episodic. New Earth Leadership is lived through regulated transitions, not permanent transcendence. The task is not transcendence. The task is integration. A psycopomp does not pull people out of the world; they guide people back into it, changed but intact. I teach how to stabilize, to hold the container's capacity without collapsing under pressure.

In the Egyptian Mystery traditions, this role was embodied by Anubis, the guide of souls. Anubis presided over thresholds—death, judgment, transformation—and taught surrender not as weakness, but as intelligence. He is often depicted hanging upside down, symbolizing the inversion required at moments of transition. At thresholds, the question is no longer *why is this happening to me?*' but rather *what is this asking of me, and how is this happening for me?*'

In 2012, during a period of deep seal activation and initiation work, I experienced my first direct transmission from Thoth, who imparted foundational knowledge of protection, stability, and integrity—preparing me for the shamanic teachings that would follow through the Neteru. In time, Anubis entered my field, guiding me through direct training in liminal navigation, nervous-system stabilization, and energetic surgery. Thoth's given name is D'Jehuti, pronounced Tehuti. He came in first as the God of Scribe, Knowledge, Wisdom, and Divine Order. Then, Ra is who trained me for 6 months during meditation and dreams. He taught me how to stay cool under pressure. As the son of Osiris, god of death and resurrection, Anubis holds the passage between worlds. I have been told—and have come to know through lived experience—that I serve as a gatekeeper to Osiris, holding a bridge between the upper worlds and the lower world, the death and rebirth of the old identity to the new one, Life and death, soul and ego, trauma and healing, fragmentation and wholeness. The bridge can be described as the human consciousness between the 5D upper world and the 3D lower world. My work is to help the spirit leave and re-enter the body safely, without overwhelming the human system. Simply put, the nervous system is the living bridge between the (3D) physical and (5D) spiritual world. And at the heart of the bridge runs the vagus nerve, the pathway that tells the body whether it is safe to open to a higher state of consciousness. I was chosen for this work many lifetimes ago; my soul completed its journey and ascended, and it made a conscious decision to return here to help other humans during this time of mass awakening. I did not step into this role solely based on theory, philosophy, or spiritual study. I was initiated through collapse.

The third initiation develops the capacity for emotional containment, allowing individuals to feel fully without being overtaken. In this work, shadow integration is not approached through catharsis, analysis, or forced release. Instead, it is rooted in containment—the nervous system's ability to remain present with emotional truth without collapsing, dissociating, or projecting. Many people avoid emotional depth because their system lacks this capacity; others plunge into it and become overwhelmed. This step creates a middle path where truth can be met safely. The amount of consciousness that can be held by your body, is the truth.

Practices in this initiation emphasize body-based emotional tracking rather than narrative processing. Feelings are experienced as sensations, movements, or energetic shifts, without immediately attaching stories or judgments. Pendulation between sensation and regulation teaches the system how to touch intensity and return to safety, gradually expanding emotional capacity. Patterns are witnessed with neutrality rather than self-attack, allowing previously split-off aspects of the psyche to reintegrate organically. Over time, the nervous system learns that emotional truth does not equal danger. The results of this work are profound. Emotional maturity replaces reactivity, and projection decreases as individuals take responsibility for their internal states. Compassion deepens—not as an ideal, but as a natural outcome of integration. Previously exiled parts of the self return, restoring vitality and coherence. Rather than being ruled by unprocessed emotion, individuals gain choice and responsiveness.

In New Earth Leadership, this capacity is non-negotiable. An unintegrated shadow cannot sustain a collective rooted in unity. Leaders, healers, and community members must be able to hold complexity without collapsing into polarity or blame. Emotional containment allows individuals to engage difference, conflict, and transformation without reverting to survival responses. This step supports the emergence of mature, integrated humans capable of co-creating a coherent collective reality.

The fourth initiation fully awakens the body through somatic integration. At this stage, awareness is no longer something one accesses during practice and leaves behind afterward; it begins to reorganize posture, breath, movement, and voice. Awakening becomes lived rather than conceptual. This step addresses the common gap where insight exists without embodiment, leading to instability or exhaustion. Somatic integration works by allowing awareness to reshape the body's habitual patterns gently. Postural awareness reveals where tension, bracing, or collapse has been held for protection. Breath and movement practices invite the nervous system to release chronic holding, while vocal toning supports regulation through resonance. Interrupted survival responses—fight, flight, freeze—are completed slowly and safely, allowing stored energy to discharge without retraumatization. Somatic integration helps reshape neuroperception and the autonomic nervous system. Stillness after release is emphasized to ensure integration rather than overstimulation. As coherence increases, chronic tension diminishes and vitality returns. The body begins to feel like a supportive home rather than an obstacle. Presence deepens, and the nervous system settles into a regulated baseline that no longer requires constant effort to maintain. Embodied stability allows awareness to remain present through daily life, not just during spiritual practice.

In the context of New Earth Leadership, somatic integration is how consciousness anchors into the physical plane. A new paradigm cannot be sustained through ideas alone—it must be lived through coherent bodies. This step ensures that expanded awareness becomes embodied wisdom, allowing humans to act, relate, and create from regulation rather than compensation. New Earth is not ascended away from the body; it is embodied through it. From that moment on, my path became clear: *awakening without embodiment destabilizes*. Consciousness must land in a stabilized nervous system to be lived. What I came to understand—first through experience and later through study—is that awakening does not occur in the conscious mind first. It appears in the subconscious, and the subconscious does not speak in language or belief. Its programming is shaped by the vagus nerve and the autonomic nervous system, which continuously register states of being through feelings and sensations. Experiences of pain, joy, peace, love, fear, and connection are encoded in bodily states and serve as templates through which life is interpreted. The vagus nerve transmits signals for sensation, rhythm, posture, reflexes, and state, forming the foundation of what we might call neuroception—the nervous system's unconscious perception of safety or danger. Most human behavior is shaped here, below the level of awareness. When neuroception registers threat, even subtly, it drives reactions and patterns that later appear as unwanted conscious behaviors, emotional reactivity, avoidance, or relational conflict. People often believe they are making conscious choices, while in reality, the subconscious nervous system is guiding behavior to maintain safety.

The subconscious is not a storehouse of hidden thoughts; it is the body's survival intelligence. It lives in breath patterns, muscle tone, gut sensation, heart rhythm, and the instinctive movements toward or away from life. Before the mind asks whether something is true, the subconscious asks only one question: *Am I safe?* Safety is why so many awakenings destabilize people. Insight arrives faster than safety. Consciousness expands, but the subconscious—whose function is protection—has not yet learned that it can survive what opening reveals. When safety is absent, expansion is interpreted as a threat. Anxiety, dissociation, emotional flooding, or shutdown are not spiritual failures; they are biological responses. The soul may be ready, but the subconscious has not yet learned that the body can hold the light. When the vagus nerve is regulated, the body enters a state of safety and connection, and spiritual practice becomes embodied rather than escapist. Meditation no longer leads to dissociation. Channeling does not require leaving the body. Emotion can move without overwhelming the system. Altered states can be entered and exited with clarity, and consciousness can rise without losing the capacity to return. This understanding was never absent in ancient initiatory traditions. In Egypt and other mystery schools, initiation was gradual, embodied, and somatic. The temples trained the body to receive divinity, not escape from human experience. The nervous system was prepared so that expanded consciousness could be lived, not merely glimpsed.

As a psychopomp, my work lives precisely at this threshold. I do not work only with insight or energy; I work with state. I track the nervous system as someone enters the unknown. I watch breath, posture, tone, and orientation. Holding the bridge means remaining regulated while another person's identity reorganizes, while their subconscious searches for safety, and while their nervous system learns it can survive a deeper truth. This is why integration cannot be rushed. Awakening is not conceptual. It is physiological. The body must learn safety where it once learned protection. When the subconscious is met with safety again and again—through breath, sound, rhythm, orientation, and regulated presence—it reorganizes. Old survival responses soften, perception shifts, and consciousness can finally stabilize in the body. This is the culmination of the journey: Step Five of this program—the initiation of embodiment—where awakening becomes livable, sustainable, and integrated into ordinary human life. And this final step is not achieved through insight alone, but through repetition. Practice. Practice. Practice.

The fifth initiation establishes coherent presence and transmission, where the regulated nervous system itself becomes stabilizing to others. At this stage, presence replaces effort. One does not attempt to transmit energy, healing, or teaching—coherence naturally entrains the field. This is not performance or technique; it is embodiment. This step works through state-based reprogramming rather than cognitive affirmation. Sound, rhythm, and frequency imprint coherence at the nervous system level, while identity becomes anchored in felt regulation rather than roles or effort. Presence is trained as a physiological state, not a personality trait. Over time, the system learns to maintain coherence under pressure, allowing intuition to arise without anxiety and leadership to emerge without force. The results are subtle but unmistakable. Presence becomes calming and stabilizing to others. Leadership feels natural rather than effortful. Spiritual practice becomes sustainable because it is no longer draining the system. Intuition flows cleanly, and action arises from clarity rather than urgency. The individual becomes a point of coherence within their environment. In New Earth Leadership, this is how consciousness spreads—not through ideology, but through entrainment. New Earth Leadership is not taught; it is transmitted through regulated presence. As more individuals embody coherence, the collective field shifts organically. This initiation represents the mature expression of stabilized awakening: becoming the bridge that spirit can trust to move through the human world.

Although I owned a gym and coached many performers, athletes, and artists, I discovered one consistent truth: intention, stability, and consistency create results. This is the same foundational principle of the Living Bridge—you must set a clear intention, create internal stability, and remain consistent in your practice for transformation to occur. While building and operating the gym, my spiritual path was unfolding in parallel. As early as 2008, I began receiving activation work and initiations during deep meditation, opening the doorway into deeper energetic and spiritual understanding. These early experiences laid the foundation for what would later become my life's work. Through sacred seal work and ceremonies in 2012 I had direct encounters with the Egyptian Neteru—Thoth, Ra, Sekhmet, and Anubis—I was trained in energetic surgery, sound codes, entity removal, sacred language, and liminal navigation. These experiences refined my ability to guide others through profound states of healing and transformation. By 2015, I began leading weekly guided meditations—often after the gym closed—bridging the worlds of physical training and inner transformation. What started as intimate sessions quickly revealed the power of combining nervous system regulation, intention, and altered states of consciousness. In 2016, I formalized my work by becoming a certified hypnotherapist, further expanding into NLP and Time Line Therapy. From there, my training deepened through initiations and studies within Egyptian Mystery traditions, Hermetic lineages, Delphi University, Atlantean Mystery School teachings, and advanced sound and hypnotic sciences. Over time, I became a Reiki Master, ordained minister, Doctor of Divinity In Spiritual Healing Arts, a medium, and a specialist in nervous system stabilization and subconscious reprogramming. For over 15 years, I have guided thousands of individuals through trance, healing, and deep integration—helping them build the internal safety, awareness, and consistency required to embody lasting transformation.

Through this work, one law revealed itself above all others: awakening cannot skip embodiment. Awareness must become lived regulation, not merely expanded perception. This realization led to the creation of The Living Bridge, a ten to fifteen-week initiation into self for those who have already awakened and now feel the call to stabilize what has opened. The nervous system is the container for consciousness. When regulation deepens, intuition sharpens. When safety returns to the body, awareness settles naturally. Rather than chasing higher states, people begin inhabiting them. Insight becomes lived. Peace becomes embodied. This same principle forms the foundation of my work, *The Living Bridge,* which trains individuals to remain awake in a human body on a living Earth during a time of rapid collective change. Many sense the emergence of a New Earth Leadership, yet humanity's nervous system has been shaped by trauma, urgency, and survival. Without stabilization, even high-frequency states become unsustainable.

New Earth consciousness is not sustained by belief alone. It is sustained by regulated bodies, coherent nervous systems, and hearts that can remain open without collapse. The Egyptians understood this. Consciousness was trained to descend, not escape. As a psycopomp and shaman, I guide those who are stuck in liminal space—between old identity and new embodiment—using sound, breath, meditation, hypnosis, education, and, when appropriate, plant medicine. My work is for those who have crossed a threshold but have not yet returned home to themselves and those that need to cross the next threshold to go to the next level but are in a liminal state. Awakening is no longer a phase. It becomes a stabilized way of being and living. Awakening is not an escape from Earth. It is learning how to belong to her again, fully and safely.

I am seated on the Council of New Earth Leadership not because I seek higher states, but because I stabilize them. My role is to ensure that consciousness expansion does not outpace the human system's capacity to hold it. I am not a peak-state teacher. I am a capacity builder, a bridge-holder between ancient wisdom and modern nervous-system science, between spirit and biology, between heaven and Earth. Many can open portals. Very few can hold the crossing. That is my dharma. That is my role. And that is why I have my seat on the Council of New Earth Leadership.

Derek Taylor

Self-Mastery Coach & Spiritual Awakening Guide.

Derek "Shaman Rah" Taylor DD is a spiritual teacher, nervous system specialist, and transformational guide helping individuals achieve self-mastery through embodied self-love, awareness, and authentic expression. His work is rooted in the understanding that real change begins in the nervous system—by creating internal safety, people can access their truth and fully embody who they are becoming.

With over fifteen years of experience, Rah supports spiritual awakening and personal transformation by teaching nervous system regulation, emotional stability, and freedom from subconscious survival patterns. His approach blends ancient spiritual wisdom with modern modalities such as hypnosis, NLP, timeline therapy, somatic practices, and sound healing.

Rah emphasizes that self-love is a regulated state, self-awareness is safe integration, and self-expression flows naturally when the body no longer perceives threat. He holds a Doctorate of Divinity, is a Certified Hypnotherapist, NLP Practitioner, and Timeline Therapy Practitioner, and works as an ordained minister, medium, and shaman.

Through his signature programs, including *The Violet Flame: Karmic Alchemy* and the *Living Bridge Method*, Rah teaches individuals how to stabilize the nervous system, clear emotional and energetic blockages, and reprogram limiting beliefs—allowing them to live with clarity, purpose, peace, and power. His mission is to help people not just awaken, but to feel safe enough to stay awakened, embodied, and fully expressed in their lives in the most authentic way.

⊕ www.shamanrah.com

◎ @oraclestouch

Scan QR code to learn more about Derek Taylor.

Livia
Devi

Chapter 8

Born Behind the Iron Curtain, Called to Lead a New Earth

"We will not vote the New Earth into existence.
We will not legislate it or fund it into being.
We will embody it, one conscious leader at a time."

\- Livia Devi

I was born in Romania under the communist regime of Nicolae Ceaușescu, a system that defined leadership through control, surveillance, and centralized power rather than through service, accountability, or human dignity. In that environment, private property was severely restricted, freedom of speech was dangerous, and personal autonomy existed within narrow and carefully monitored boundaries. To understand life in Romania before the 1989 Revolution is to understand a society shaped not only by political control, but by a deep and pervasive psychological conditioning that reached into every corner of ordinary life.

The state controlled employment, housing, food distribution, media, and education, and basic necessities were rationed while electricity and heat were frequently restricted during harsh winters. Long lines formed for bread, oil, sugar, and meat. Information was filtered through state propaganda, and the secret police — the Securitate — maintained an extensive surveillance network, recruiting informants and cultivating an atmosphere of distrust that penetrated neighborhoods, workplaces, and even families. Fear did not always manifest as visible oppression; it lived in anticipation, in the space between what was said and what was meant, in the careful calculation of who was listening and what they might report.

People learned to speak cautiously, to avoid political discussions in public spaces, and to lower their voices even within private homes. Children were taught what not to repeat outside the household, and criticism of the regime could result in interrogation, loss of employment, forced relocation, imprisonment, or worse. Some individuals disappeared into detention facilities, others were sentenced to forced labor until death, and stories circulated quietly about people taken away by militia cars after speaking too openly or expressing dissent. Whether every detail was known or not, the message was unmistakable: truth could cost you your safety. During the final decade of the regime, Ceaușescu's austerity policies — imposed to repay foreign debt — intensified this hardship, as food shortages worsened, heating was limited, medical supplies grew scarce, and entire communities endured deprivation while the state promoted an image of national prosperity.

The human cost of authoritarian control culminated in December 1989, when protests began in Timișoara and spread rapidly across the country as ordinary citizens demanded freedom, dignity, and an end to decades of repression. Demonstrators were met with military force, live ammunition was used against unarmed crowds, hundreds were killed, thousands were wounded, and countless families were forever marked by loss. When the regime collapsed, the revolution left deep scars not only physical and political, but psychological, and I was only seven years old, an age when a child's world should feel predictable and safe, when I witnessed scenes no child should ever see.

I remember the tension in the air, the urgency in adult voices, the sound of sirens and the abrupt silences that followed. I remember being pulled indoors and warned to stay away from windows, sensing fear before I could understand its cause, and I remember seeing men lying in the street, their bodies still, surrounded by pools of blood. Even now, the memory lives not as a single image but as a feeling — confusion, shock, and the sudden awareness that the world could become dangerous without warning. I did not yet understand politics, ideology, or revolution, but I understood fear. I understood that something irreversible was happening, and I understood that the adults around me were afraid in a way I had never seen before.

For many Romanian children of that generation, the revolution was not an abstract historical event, but a formative psychological imprint, marking the end of one system while not instantly dissolving the fear that system had cultivated. That fear lingered in homes, in conversations spoken in lowered voices, in the reflex to avoid visibility, in the instinct to stay safe by staying silent. The fall of the regime brought freedom, but freedom arrived into a society shaped by decades of control, scarcity, and surveillance, and trust could not be rebuilt overnight because courage, too, had to be relearned.

For me, the memory of that winter became more than a childhood trauma; it became an early awareness of the consequences of power without accountability and governance without humanity.

I would spend many years understanding what I had witnessed, but even then, something within me recognized a simple truth: systems shape lives, and when systems lose their moral center, ordinary people bear the cost. That awareness would later become one of the quiet forces guiding my path toward understanding leadership, responsibility, and the human impact of power.

The fall of communism ended the system, but it did not erase the imprint it left on the collective psyche. Generational trauma does not disappear with a change of government, it lingers in habits of caution, in distrust of institutions, in fear of authority, and in a subconscious belief that safety lies in conformity rather than expression. Even today, decades later, remnants of that conditioning remain visible in how people relate to power, opportunity, and self-expression, because many learned to survive by not standing out, learned that initiative could attract risk and learned that silence ensured safety, and these patterns shaped not only behavior but identity itself.

And yet, within my home, another reality existed. Despite material scarcity, my parents cultivated an environment rooted in dignity, ethical clarity, and inner freedom. We were not wealthy in financial terms, but I was raised with an understanding that true wealth begins within, in values, integrity, education, and the courage to think independently. They spoke of freedom not only as a political condition but as an inner state that no regime could confiscate, and they taught me that self-respect does not depend on external validation, that knowledge creates opportunity, and that personal responsibility is itself a form of power. While the outer world operated through fear and limitation, they nurtured courage and possibility, and these early lessons shaped my relationship with leadership long before I consciously chose that path.

What sustained many families during those years was not access to opportunity, but the quiet preservation of inner freedom. My parents, like most people living under communism, had never traveled beyond the borders of Romania, had never experienced the open movement, civic liberties, or economic possibilities that existed elsewhere, and yet they carried within them an intuitive understanding that life could be larger than the circumstances imposed upon it. They could not point to foreign cities they had seen or freedoms they had personally exercised, but they held an inner orientation toward dignity, self-respect, and possibility that expressed itself in subtle yet powerful ways. They refused to allow scarcity to define our imagination or fear to dictate our choices, speaking carefully in public as everyone did, yet cultivating within our home a language of trust, curiosity, and quiet courage. They taught my sister and me that our worth was not determined by the limitations around us, encouraged us to think independently and question respectfully, and reinforced the belief that intellectual freedom and personal integrity could not be confiscated, even when resources were scarce.

Looking back, I recognize that they transmitted something far more valuable than material security: they transmitted psychological and emotional sovereignty, helping us reinterpret our environment not as a prison, but as a starting point, teaching us to see constraint without internalizing it. While many families, shaped by years of surveillance and scarcity, adopted protective caution as a survival strategy, my parents quietly cultivated resilience and possibility, acknowledging limitations while encouraging us never to become defined by them. They did not deny reality; they contextualized it, and this reframing shaped our trajectory in ways I only understood much later in my adult life.

As Romania transitioned out of communism, this difference in inner orientation became increasingly visible. Many of the children and adolescents I grew up, with carried forward a deeply conditioned fear of risk, because years of collective control had instilled a subconscious association between visibility and danger, initiative and punishment, ambition and vulnerability, and even in freedom, hesitation remained. Some of my classmates were exceptionally intelligent and capable, yet the inherited caution of their families and communities shaped their choices — they avoided uncertainty, remained within familiar boundaries, and chose stability over exploration, staying in the same small town where we grew up not because they lacked talent, but because leaving felt unsafe at a level deeper than conscious reasoning. Fear had outlived the system that produced it.

My sister and I, by contrast, had been encouraged to explore beyond the horizon we could see, taught that opportunity required courage, that growth required movement, and that dignity required self-trust. We pursued our studies, our passions, and our ambitions with a sense of permission that did not come from the state but from the emotional environment created within our family, and this did not eliminate fear so much as transform our relationship to it — learning to interpret uncertainty not as danger but as possibility, learning that risk is inherent in growth and that freedom is not merely political but psychological.

Only later did I fully appreciate how extraordinary this inheritance was. My parents had never experienced external freedom in the ways they hoped for us, yet they safeguarded its essence within their values, their parenting, and their quiet defiance of resignation. They could not give us a different system, but they gave us a different lens, and that lens shaped our choices in ways that no regime could have predicted. It also revealed something essential about leadership: systems influence behavior, but inner orientation determines destiny, and even under constraint, individuals and families can cultivate resilience, vision, and courage becoming the bridge between inherited limitations and emerging possibilities, not only for their children but for the societies those children will one day help shape.

When Romania transitioned out of communism, hope surged across the nation, and democracy promised transparency, opportunity, and integration into the broader European community. Like many of my generation, I believed in rebuilding systems rooted in fairness and accountability, and I pursued higher education at the National School of Political Science and Administrative Studies, seeking to understand governance, policy, and institutional design, later completing a master's degree in European Law out of a conviction that legal frameworks and democratic structures could support justice, human rights, and economic opportunity. My path was driven not only by ambition but by a genuine desire to understand how systems shape freedom and human dignity.

For a brief period, I worked within the government, eager to contribute to Romania's democratic evolution, yet within six months, I encountered a reality that challenged my idealism in ways I had not anticipated. While the political system had changed, remnants of old patterns persisted: bureaucracy slowed progress, informal influence networks shaped decisions beneath the surface, nepotism and favoritism often overshadowed merit, and transparency existed in principle but not always in practice. I began to see that systems may change faster than mindsets, that authoritarian structures can fall while hierarchical thinking, fear-based decision-making, and distrust remain embedded in institutional culture and collective psychology. This realization marked a turning point in my understanding of leadership, because I understood that true transformation cannot be achieved through structural reform alone — laws can change, governments can transition, institutions can be redesigned, but if consciousness does not evolve, the same patterns reappear in new forms.

Growing up under authoritarian control had taught me the cost of suppressed freedom, while the values instilled by my parents had taught me that leadership begins within — in integrity, responsibility, and the courage to think independently. These experiences shaped my later mission: to explore leadership not merely as authority or governance but as consciousness, responsibility, and ethical stewardship, because leadership is not only about how systems are designed but about how human beings think, relate, and choose. When fear shapes consciousness, leadership reproduces control, but when awareness shapes consciousness, leadership can cultivate freedom, and the work of evolving leadership is therefore not only political or institutional it is psychological, cultural, deeply human, and it begins within.

Witnessing these realities within government institutions confronted me with a difficult truth: structural change alone does not guarantee ethical leadership, and if the structures entrusted with serving the public were not embodying the principles they proclaimed, I needed to understand where influence truly resided and how systems of power actually functioned in the modern world. I had spent seven years preparing for a career within governmental and European institutional structures, and letting go of that path was neither impulsive nor easy — it required releasing not only professional ambition but also an identity I had worked diligently to build, yet clarity leaves little room for compromise.

I began to recognize that governments do not operate in isolation, that behind policies, regulatory frameworks, and global agreements stand economic forces, multinational corporations, financial institutions, and market dynamics that shape decision-making at every level, and to understand leadership in its contemporary form, I felt called to move closer to the economic engines that influence global systems. With both uncertainty and resolve, I stepped away from the career I had prepared for and began again this time in the corporate world.

Leaving that path was not simply a professional decision; it was an identity rupture. For seven years, I had oriented my life toward public service, governance, and the belief that institutional reform could strengthen democracy and protect human dignity, and to step away from it meant relinquishing more than a career plan — it meant releasing a version of myself I had worked diligently to become. Many people remain on paths that no longer align with their deeper truth because the identity attached to those paths feels safer than the uncertainty of change: titles confer belonging, institutions confer legitimacy, and predictable roles provide social recognition and psychological security. Walking away can feel like stepping into invisibility, and yet growth rarely occurs inside identities we have outgrown.

When I chose to leave the governmental track and begin again in the corporate world, it was not because the decision felt comfortable but because clarity had made staying more difficult than leaving. From the outside, the decision appeared counterintuitive. I was abandoning a path associated with stability, prestige, and public service in favor of an uncertain beginning in an entirely different environment — and many would not make such a choice, because years of preparation create momentum, and stepping away from that momentum requires confronting fear, uncertainty, and the opinions of others. But identity is not meant to be a cage; it is meant to be a phase in our evolution, and what I did not fully understand at the time but recognize now is that identity shifts precede life shifts, and when we release an identity that no longer reflects who we are becoming, we create space for a new reality to emerge.

This process can feel disorienting because our sense of self reorganizes before external results appear — we stand in an in-between space, no longer who we were, not yet who we are becoming, and this threshold is precisely where transformation begins. Changing professional direction required more than acquiring new skills; it required recalibrating my internal orientation entirely. In government environments, influence often moved through institutional hierarchy and policy frameworks, while in corporate environments it flowed through performance, strategic value, and economic outcomes, demanding different languages, different rhythms, and different ways of thinking. To adapt, I had to expand beyond the identity I had constructed, learning to navigate new cultural norms, interpret new metrics of success, and operate within systems driven by speed, competition, and measurable results, while beneath these adaptations a deeper process unfolded — learning to remain anchored in my values while moving within unfamiliar structures, understanding that identity transformation does not require abandoning one's essence but refining it.

In retrospect, this decision marked one of the most significant thresholds of my life, requiring the courage to step away from external validation and the humility to begin again, asking me to trust that growth often demands disorientation and that clarity sometimes emerges only after we release what once felt certain. Many individuals feel an inner call to change direction, yet remain constrained by fear of losing status, security, or recognition, but transformation asks a deeper question: are we loyal to our identity, or to our evolution? Every time we choose evolution, we expand the field of possibility available to us, and what we often interpret as risk is, in truth, movement toward alignment — alignment that generates a reality shift, clarity that generates momentum. From a broader perspective, identity shifts represent more than career transitions; they signal a shift in consciousness, because when we change how we see ourselves, we change how we perceive opportunity, how we engage with challenge, and how we interpret uncertainty, and our external reality begins to reorganize around our internal orientation. My transition from the governmental path into the corporate world was not an abandonment of purpose; it was a reconfiguration of it.

I was starting from the beginning in a new environment, a new culture, and a new professional paradigm, yet beneath the uncertainty lived a clear intention: I wanted to understand the architecture of power from the inside, to learn how decisions were made, how influence moved, and how leadership functioned within systems that shape economies, labor, and global markets.

Over the next fifteen years working in corporate America, I witnessed another form of conditioning — more subtle than authoritarian control, yet equally influential in shaping behavior, identity, and leadership.

If communism had conditioned citizens through fear and scarcity, corporate culture often conditioned individuals through competition, performance metrics, and the relentless pursuit of growth, measuring success in quarterly results, market share, and shareholder value, and making efficiency, productivity, and scalability the dominant priorities.

Leadership development in this world emphasized performance optimization, strategic dominance, and competitive positioning, and on the surface, these models appeared meritocratic and opportunity-driven, rewarding ambition and results, promoting those who could deliver measurable outcomes.

Yet beneath this framework, I began to observe patterns that limited human potential rather than expanded it, as competition was frequently prioritized over collaboration, short-term gains overshadowed long-term stewardship, and individual advancement often took precedence over collective well-being.

Burnout was normalized as dedication, and human value became linked to performance metrics. While these systems generated innovation and economic growth, they also cultivated environments where fear of failure, pressure to outperform peers, and the constant demand for measurable productivity shaped behavior and decision-making in ways that gradually eroded trust and coherence.

People learned to protect their roles rather than share knowledge, teams competed internally for recognition and resources, and creativity narrowed under pressure to produce predictable results.

Leadership often became synonymous with authority, control, and performance management rather than vision, empathy, and human development. Even well-intentioned leaders found themselves operating within structures that rewarded compliance over courage and efficiency over reflection, because the system itself shaped behavior, reinforcing patterns of competition, scarcity thinking, and emotional disconnection regardless of individual intention.

I began to recognize a familiar dynamic: while the mechanisms differed, both authoritarian regimes and hyper-competitive corporate systems could condition individuals to disconnect from their inner voice in order to conform to external expectations, one system governing through fear of punishment and the other through fear of inadequacy, one restricting freedom through political control and the other through performance pressure and an identity tied to achievement, with neither model fully honoring the wholeness of the human being.

This realization did not diminish the value of enterprise, innovation, or economic development; rather, it illuminated the need for a more evolved model of leadership.

One that integrates performance with purpose, strategy with ethics, and success with human sustainability

These years became a second education - not in theory, but in lived systems — revealing how power operates within modern economies, how culture shapes decision-making, and how leadership models influence human behavior at scale, and most importantly, revealing that true transformation will not come from replacing one system with another but from evolving the consciousness that informs them both.

It became clear to me that the future of leadership must transcend the binaries of past systems — beyond authoritarian control and beyond purely competitive paradigms — toward models rooted in responsibility, collaboration, ethical clarity, and human dignity, because leadership is not merely about directing outcomes but about shaping the conditions in which human potential can flourish. And that understanding would eventually lead me toward the work I am now called to do.

As my professional life continued to evolve, another dimension of transformation began to unfold, one that did not arise from strategic planning, intellectual pursuit, or career ambition, but from an event that arrived with a force and mystery my conscious mind had no framework to understand.

Until that time, spirituality and expanded states of awareness were not part of my worldview; my life was structured, analytical, and results-driven, and I was serving in an executive role within a major IT company, responsible for global teams, complex operations, and high-stakes decision-making, with my days defined by metrics, performance targets, and strategic outcomes.

I trusted logic, discipline, and efficiency, and consciousness, energy, or multidimensional awareness were not concepts I explored.

Then, in 2016, something happened that dissolved the boundaries of everything I believed reality to be. One morning, before dawn, I woke up to lead an international conference call with more than twenty people I managed, and as I prepared to begin, I suddenly lost consciousness and collapsed onto the couch. When I regained awareness nearly an hour later, I encountered a state of perception unlike anything I had known. My mind was filled with an immense influx of internal sound, as though countless voices were speaking simultaneously, with no single message, only a vast field of noise, layered and overwhelming, where I could not distinguish language or meaning but only intensity and presence.

My logical mind moved quickly to interpret the experience through the frameworks it knew, and I contacted my direct manager and attempted to explain what I was experiencing, assuming I was facing severe burnout or neurological overload.

The days that followed dismantled that assumption, as my family doctor could not identify a medical cause, and as the experience continued, I found myself confronting a reality that existed outside conventional explanations.

Eventually, a friend gave me the contact details of a psychiatrist whose presence I can only describe as divinely guided, someone who approached my condition not with fear or pathology, but with steadiness, compassion, and an understanding that extended beyond traditional clinical frameworks.

Rather than diagnosing illness, he introduced the possibility of awakening, a word that at the time meant nothing to me. My company granted me six months of medical leave while continuing my salary and benefits, allowing me the space to recover and seek understanding without the pressure of immediate return, and during this period, I met weekly with the psychiatrist, who gently introduced me to concepts of consciousness expansion, psychological integration, and the unfolding of awareness beyond conditioned identity.

Gradually, the overwhelming internal noise began to organize itself into coherent streams of perception, and over time, I perceived four distinct layers within my inner awareness: my higher self, my ego struggling to maintain familiar identity structures, and two streams of intelligence communicating not through words but through direct knowledge.

As the process deepened, these intelligences identified themselves as the 12D Sirian Council of Light and the 7D Arcturian Council of Light. At the time, I had no prior exposure to these names or concepts, and my analytical mind would not have invented them, nor did I possess any spiritual framework through which to interpret the experience, yet the clarity, coherence, and intelligence conveyed through these transmissions felt precise, structured, and profoundly benevolent.

From early 2016 through February 2017, I underwent what can only be described as an accelerated period of consciousness expansion under the guidance of the 12D Sirian Council of Light — a period that functioned as a multidimensional training, dismantling perceptual limitations and reorganizing my understanding of reality, awareness, and human potential.

The pace of this transformation was extraordinary, as insights unfolded with a velocity that seemed to compress decades of spiritual study, psychological integration, and philosophical inquiry into a single year, introducing me to principles that bridged quantum physics, multidimensional awareness, energetic coherence, interdimensional perception, and the architecture of consciousness itself, while what many pursue over decades of disciplined spiritual practice unfolded in a concentrated initiation that reshaped my awareness from the inside out.

This process was not abstract; it required emotional integration, psychological recalibration, nervous system regulation, and the dissolution of identity structures that could not coexist with expanded perception. While at times it was disorienting and at times profoundly illuminating, it was always transformative.

By February 2017, this phase of training reached completion, my consciousness had stabilized into a new coherence, and I was guided into the next stage of service: becoming a trance- channel for the 7D Arcturian Council of Light. This was not something I had sought; it was something I had been prepared for. Through this process, I came to understand that consciousness is not confined to the individual mind, and that human awareness has access to fields of intelligence far beyond the conditioning of personality and culture, and that such experiences are not an escape from reality but an expansion of it.

With reverence and certainty, I resigned from my corporate position and stepped into an entirely new chapter of my life, one devoted not only to systems transformation and leadership evolution, but to the expansion of human consciousness itself.

Looking back, what once felt inexplicable now reveals itself as a sacred threshold. At the time, my conscious mind could not comprehend what was unfolding, yet today I understand that transformation often arrives before understanding, and that the deepest initiations of our lives begin beyond the boundaries of what we believe to be possible. This experience taught me that true transformation does not originate outside us; it emerges from within, dissolving old structures, expanding perception, and inviting us into deeper coherence with who we truly are.

The year of quantum and multidimensional training that unfolded between early 2016 and February 2017 did not simply expand my awareness; it dismantled the unconscious architecture through which I had previously perceived reality, as layers of inherited conditioning, cultural programming, survival responses, and identity constructs began to surface and dissolve, and beliefs I had never consciously examined revealed themselves as internal structures shaping perception and behavior. Patterns rooted in fear, performance conditioning, scarcity consciousness, and external validation loosened their hold — not through intellectual process but through direct experience, cellular and embodied, feeling as though the operating system through which I understood myself and the world was being rewritten from within. At times, memories surfaced without emotional charge; at other times, deep-seated patterns dissolved with a quiet finality, leaving behind a sense of spaciousness I had never known, and identities that once felt essential - professional roles, cultural expectations, performance-based self-worth — no longer defined my sense of being. What remained was presence, clarity, and an awareness unburdened by the reflexive conditioning of the past.

Through this process, I came to understand that much of what we consider personality is a composite of adaptation, protection, and social conditioning, and when these layers soften, something more essential becomes accessible — an inner coherence not shaped by fear, comparison, or external validation.

As this reorganization stabilized, my perception shifted from fragmentation toward integration, my mind began processing information differently, and patterns, systems, and relationships between seemingly unrelated fields of knowledge became visible with striking clarity, as complex data organized itself into coherent frameworks and insights arrived not as linear reasoning but as fully formed understanding.

During this period, my connection with the 7D Arcturian Council of Light deepened into what I experienced as an interface with a field of intelligence oriented toward coherence, harmonic balance, and the evolution of human consciousness.

It became clear that my role was not to replace my individuality but to become a clear and coherent vessel through which higher-order intelligence, compassion, and transformative insight could be translated into practical application, serving as a bridge that translates expanded awareness into grounded, actionable guidance supporting human growth and evolution.

The term "vessel of light," as I understand it, does not imply passivity; it implies coherence, a nervous system regulated enough, a psyche integrated enough, and an awareness clear enough to transmit insight without distortion from fear, ego defense, or unconscious programming. From this coherence emerged a new capacity: the ability to hold and organize vast amounts of information, perceive systemic patterns quickly, and translate complex multidimensional insights into practical strategies for human development and leadership evolution.

In my work with individuals and leaders, this integration allows me to accelerate clarity, reveal unseen patterns, and support rapid transformation, as people often describe gaining in months what previously felt inaccessible for years, not because something is given to them, but because what already exists within them is activated.

When individuals reconnect with their inner coherence, their lives often reorganize rapidly: decisions become clearer, relationships shift, career paths realign, health improves, creativity expands, and purpose becomes actionable, because transformation accelerates not when something external is imposed but when inner fragmentation dissolves.

Over time, this work evolved into supporting New Earth Leaders and Light Leaders individuals across sectors who feel called to lead with integrity, consciousness, and responsibility in a rapidly changing world, working in government, corporations, education, healthcare, innovation, or community systems, united not by profession but by a shared readiness to lead from coherence rather than fear. Through this work, I have witnessed extraordinary transformations: leaders reclaiming clarity after burnout, innovators aligning vision with purpose, decision-makers integrating compassion with strategy, and individuals stepping into roles they once believed were beyond their capacity.

What I came to understand through my own transformation is this: human potential expands when consciousness expands, leadership evolves when inner coherence replaces inner conflict, and systems transform when the individuals within them awaken to clarity and responsibility. This phase of my evolution did not remove me from the world; it prepared me to serve within it with greater clarity, deeper compassion, and an expanded capacity to support transformation at both individual and systemic levels.

What I have come to understand, looking back across the arc of my life, is that I did not move through one leadership system but through a sequence of paradigms, each of which shaped my understanding of power, responsibility, and human potential, and each of which, in its own way, revealed both what leadership can build and what it can destroy when separated from conscience, humanity, and an expanded awareness of consequence.

The first model I encountered was leadership as control — embedded in the communist regime of Nicolae Ceaușescu, where authority was centralized and enforced through surveillance, restriction, and fear, where private property was limited, freedom of speech carried real danger, and personal autonomy existed only inside carefully monitored boundaries, and where the role of leadership was not to serve the people but to preserve the system, protect ideology, and maintain compliance, often at the expense of truth and human dignity.

In such an environment, governance does not simply shape laws or institutions, it shapes the nervous system of an entire population, conditioning people to equate safety with invisibility, to associate initiative with risk, to lower their voices even in private, and to internalize a form of self-censorship that can outlive the regime itself, living on as generational trauma, as inherited caution, as a subconscious hesitation to stand out or speak clearly even decades after the visible structure has fallen.

When communism collapsed and Romania moved into democracy, I stepped into a second model, one that promised transparency, fairness, and accountability through institutions, laws, and European frameworks, and because I carried a sincere belief in the possibility of structural reform, I pursued political science and European law with the hope that governance could become a vehicle for human rights, dignity, and opportunity.

Yet the reality I encountered when I entered government work revealed one of the most defining lessons of my life: that systems may change faster than consciousness, and that institutions can adopt new language while unconsciously repeating old patterns. I witnessed bureaucracy that slowed progress and obscured accountability, informal networks of influence that shaped decisions beneath the surface, and nepotism and manipulation that weakened trust and diluted the promise of democracy, and while I did not lose faith in the importance of structure, I began to see that structure alone cannot produce transformation when the minds and hearts operating within it remain conditioned by fear, self-preservation, or inherited hierarchy — because laws can be rewritten and policies redesigned, yet if the underlying psychology of leadership remains unchanged, the same dynamics reappear under a different name.

That realization led me into a third system — corporate leadership — because I began to recognize that modern governance does not operate in isolation, and that behind the visible face of politics stand economic forces, financial institutions, corporations, and market dynamics that shape what is funded, what is prioritized, what is scaled, and what is protected. And so I made a life-altering decision that many would not make, stepping away from the career I had prepared for over seven years and beginning again in the corporate world — not because it was easy, but because it was clear that if I wanted to understand power, I needed to study it where it actually moves. Over the next fifteen years in corporate America, I encountered another form of conditioning, one far subtler than the blunt force of authoritarianism yet equally influential in shaping behavior and identity, as leadership was defined through performance metrics, competition, quarterly outcomes, strategic dominance, and relentless pressure for growth.

Over time, I began to recognize a pattern that connected these systems more than it separated them, because while communism governed through fear of punishment and corporate culture often governs through fear of inadequacy, both can condition people to prioritize safety over truth and conformity over inner alignment, shaping identity through external metrics rather than inner coherence and diminishing the wholeness of the human being when leadership is reduced to power, authority, or performance rather than understood as stewardship, responsibility, and ethical care for the lives impacted by decisions.

And then, through my own awakening and the year of multidimensional training that unfolded between early 2016 and February 2017, a deeper truth emerged that reframed everything I had witnessed — that transformation does not begin in institutions but in consciousness, and that leadership, at its root, is not merely political or corporate but psychological, emotional, ethical, and energetic, because the quality of a leader's inner world shapes the quality of their decisions, the coherence of their relationships, and the culture they create around them.

I saw that when fear shapes consciousness, leadership reproduces control even when it speaks the language of progress, and when awareness shapes consciousness, leadership can cultivate freedom, integrity, and trust even within complex systems, and this is why conscious leadership became the turning point in my understanding — because it begins not with a title but with self-awareness, not with authority but with responsibility, not with domination but with coherence.

Yet even conscious leadership, as it is often discussed, is only the bridge, because what is now emerging is not simply a new leadership style but a new leadership paradigm — one that integrates what previous systems separated, and that asks us not only how to lead but who we must become in order to lead wisely in a world that is interconnected, fast-moving, and shaped by consequences that ripple across cultures, economies, and generations.

This is the threshold where New Earth Leadership begins, not as a rejection of all that came before but as an integration and an evolution beyond it, recognizing that power without ethics creates harm, that structure without consciousness creates stagnation, that performance without humanity creates fragmentation, and that awareness without grounded action cannot build what the future requires — and therefore calling forth leaders who can hold strategic intelligence and emotional intelligence in the same breath, who can build systems while honoring the human beings living inside those systems, who can innovate without extracting life from people or planet, and who can measure success not only by growth but by regeneration, dignity, and long-term stewardship.

New Earth Leadership does not ask us to abandon effectiveness; it asks us to refine it, to root it in integrity, coherence, and responsibility, so that leadership becomes not the art of controlling outcomes, but the practice of shaping the conditions in which human potential can flourish and collective futures can be protected.

In this sense, the new paradigm is not being built somewhere outside of us — it is being built through the evolution of consciousness within us, because the future will not be shaped by systems alone but by the inner maturity of those entrusted to guide them, and this, more than anything, is what my journey across these three systems has taught me: that leadership is ultimately the mirror of consciousness made visible through decision, culture, and consequence.

From this expanded understanding, the work could no longer remain personal, local, or limited in scope, as it became clear that the transformation unfolding was not about one individual, one country, or one sector of society, but about the emergence of a new leadership consciousness capable of serving a rapidly evolving world.

Since 2019, through the founding of Livia Devi Global LLC, this mission has expanded across continents, activating and supporting leaders in every major region of the globe, as individuals from Europe, North America, Latin America, Australia, and beyond began entering this field of work — often at moments of transition, responsibility, or awakening seeking not more authority but greater coherence, not more success but deeper alignment between influence and purpose.

What emerged through these years of global engagement was unmistakable: the challenges leaders face today are shared across cultures and systems, and whether guiding governments, leading corporations, building innovative enterprises, or shaping social impact initiatives, leaders are navigating unprecedented complexity while being called to integrate clarity, ethics, and human responsibility into every decision they make.

Out of this global work, a deeper structure began to crystallize, as the Council of Eight formed not as an institution of hierarchy but as a field of coherence, a collaborative alliance of leaders whose lived experience, ethical clarity, and demonstrated integrity reflect the emerging paradigm of conscious leadership.

The Council brings together voices from Romania, the United States, Canada, Ireland, Mexico, and Australia, representing diverse cultures, disciplines, and leadership environments, yet united by a shared commitment to stewarding humanity's future with wisdom, responsibility, and expanded awareness, and it exists not to centralize authority but to model collaboration beyond ego, beyond control, and beyond dominance, with each member contributing a perspective shaped by lived responsibility and transformation, creating a collective intelligence greater than any individual voice.

Together, the Council supports the activation of New Earth Leaders across sectors and continents, offering insight, frameworks, and guidance for navigating complexity while honoring human dignity, planetary stewardship, and long-term collective well-being.

Through this work, my global mission continues to unfold, to support the evolution of leadership consciousness on Earth, to activate leaders into coherence with their highest ethical responsibility, and to help build systems that honor human dignity, ecological balance, and the continuity of life for future generations.

New Earth Leadership is not a theory, a trend, or a philosophy reserved for a select few, it is an evolutionary movement emerging through individuals who are ready to lead with clarity, courage, and conscious responsibility in a world that can no longer be guided by outdated paradigms.

We are living in a threshold moment in human history, and the future will not be shaped solely by innovation, policy, or economic growth but by the consciousness of those entrusted to lead.

Through the work of this Council, the global activation of leaders, and the shared wisdom contained within these pages, a new model of leadership is no longer theoretical.

It is emerging.

It is embodied.

It is already underway.

Livia Devi

New Earth Leader, 5D Mentor, Entrepreneur.

Livia Devi leads empowering, transformative and paradigm-breaking programs and activations for the global community of entrepreneurs, conscious creators, change makers, thought leaders and influencers. Co-creating her teachings with an advanced collective consciousness from 7D, the Arcturian Council of Light, Livia is a catalyst for the New Earth and a new era of technological advancement and evolution of consciousness.

Her dedication and service to others are evident in her role as a catalyst for the emergence of embodied New Earth leaders. Those who are ready to activate their soul mission, embrace this new era of human evolution, and co-create from the heart find in Livia a mentor and guide. Her mentorship not only equips individuals with knowledge and skills but also fosters a deep sense of divine purpose and soul connection to the greater cosmic tapestry.

Through her guidance, awakened beings of light remember who they truly are in this lifetime and through all eternity, unlocking their soul mission and contributing to the expansion and elevation of the collective consciousness of humanity. With Livia's assistance, her clients are empowered to embody their roles as co-creators of a harmonious and enlightened world.

🌐 www.LiviaDevi.com
📷 @arcturianschanneling
Scan QR code to learn more about Livia Devi.

A FINAL WORD
OF GRATITUDE

There are those whose influence lives so deeply within us that it transcends time, distance, and even death. My parents, Liliana and Eugen, are among them. Though they now guide my steps from above, their presence remains woven into everything I do and everything I have become. It was their quiet courage, their dignity in the face of limitation, and their unwavering belief in a life larger than circumstance that first taught me what true leadership looks like — not from a stage or a boardroom, but from the inside of an ordinary home, in extraordinary times. Thank you, mama and tata, for never leaving. This book, and the mission it carries, is yours as much as it is mine.

CONTINUE YOUR JOURNEY
with Livia Devi & the 7D Arcturian Council of Light

The wisdom in these pages is an opening, not an ending. If you feel called to go deeper, the following programs offer immersive pathways into activation, embodiment, and your New Earth mission.

Evolve with Livia Devi

A weekly trance-channeled transmission from Livia and the 7D Arcturian Council of Light. Each session is unique and works on an energetic level. Includes live Q&As, activations, and a growing library of teachings within a limited, curated community.

Soul Mission Accelerator

A 12-week group program for visionaries and leaders ready to define and embody their Soul Mission. It guides you through five stages: clearing limiting patterns, activating your mission, stepping into aligned leadership, releasing blocks to abundance and impact, and building a real-world foundation to bring your work into the world.

Wealth Consciousness

A 6-month journey activating your mission and building a quantum-aligned business across three levels:

- 5D — Quantum Field: Activate & Architect. Your mission and business blueprint built in the quantum field, timelines collapsed into clarity.
- 4D — Bridging: Stabilise & Lock In. Your model, positioning, energy, and identity locked in place so nothing leaks when you step into the world.
- 3D — Structuring: Build & Launch. Website, offers, messaging, CRM, brand, and sales systems — built in precise detail, then launched.

The New Earth needs your light—fully activated and expressed.
These programs are portals. The next step is yours.

> *"Your business already exists in the quantum field.*
> *We are simply the architects who help you bring it home."*
> — Livia Devi & the 7D Arcturian Council of Light

🌐 www.LiviaDevi.com
📷 @arcturianschanneling

www.ingramcontent.com/pod-product-compliance
Lightning Source LLC
Chambersburg PA
CBHW050031040726
47599CB00015B/1631